FEARLESS
AND
FREE

FEARLESS

AND

FREE

HOW SMART WOMEN PIVOT AND RELAUNCH THEIR CAREERS

WENDY SACHS

AMACOM
AMERICAN MANAGEMENT ASSOCIATION
New York • Atlanta • Brussels • Chicago • Mexico City • San Francisco
Shanghai • Tokyo • Toronto • Washington, DC

Bulk discounts available. For details visit:
www.amacombooks.org/go/specialsales
Or contact special sales:
Phone: 800-250-5308
Email: specialsls@amanet.org
View all the AMACOM titles at: www.amacombooks.org

American Management Association: www.amanet.org

This publication is designed to provide accurate and authoritative information in regard to the subject matter covered. It is sold with the understanding that the publisher is not engaged in rendering legal, accounting, or other professional service. If legal advice or other expert assistance is required, the services of a competent professional person should be sought.

Library of Congress Cataloging-in-Publication Data

Names: Sachs, Wendy, author.
Title: Fearless and free : how smart women pivot and re-launch their careers
   / by Wendy Sachs.
Description: New York, NY : AMACOM, [2017]
Identifiers: LCCN 2016042354 (print) | LCCN 2016056942 (ebook) | ISBN
   9780814437698 (hardcover) | ISBN 9780814437704 (eBook)
Subjects: LCSH: Women–Vocational guidance. | Career changes. | Career
   development.
Classification: LCC HF5382.6 .S23 2017 (print) | LCC HF5382.6 (ebook) | DDC
   650.1082–dc23
LC record available at https://lccn.loc.gov/2016042354

For my mom, who raised me to be fearless and free.

And for my husband, Michael, who supports me
unconditionally at every pivot.

Acknowledgments

WRITING A BOOK IS A certain kind of madness. It's a weirdly lonely process where you can spend months, years even, in your own head hoping that what you ultimately deliver is wickedly smart, hilariously entertaining, or somehow provocative enough to make it worthy of an NPR or *Today* show segment. To say that it takes a tribe to see you through the grueling book-writing odyssey is cliché, but truly without my squad of enthusiastic cheerleaders, it may not have happened.

I am forever indebted to the inspiring women who shared and trusted me with their personal stories, heartbreaking failures, wild successes, and astute wisdom. With women, I believe that the professional and personal are almost always intermingled. I took great care in presenting the women's powerful stories, and I hope I did them the justice they deserve.

Big, heartfelt thank-yous go to Rachel Sklar, Glynnis MacNicol, and the awesome ladies from TheLi.st. Many of the stories in this book come from these exceptionally talented and generous women. Your collective enthusiasm, feedback, and advice have helped me through my book journey. From the title and cover to the offers to promote my book, your support has been immeasurable.

To my friend Jocelyn Fine, who still doesn't quite believe me when I tell her that she sparked the fire in me to write the book proposal that became this book, an idea that had marinated in my head for three years. It was Jocelyn's fierce spirit and positive energy as she fought her way through breast cancer that motivated me to stop thinking about this book and start writing it. An off-hand remark that I would be miserable if someone else writes this book before me kicked me into action. She was right. Thank you, Jocelyn, for getting me going.

We are incredibly fortunate in life when a work friend becomes a true friend. Jo Flattery, my lovely and talented former colleague—thank you for sharing your thoughts on all things "sorry" and for reading nearly every chapter of my manuscript. Your laser-sharp advice was invaluable—as is your friendship. You win the award for most dedicated unpaid editor. Two days before this book was due and I was sweating over my final chapter, desperate for feedback, you texted me from the emergency room that your son Leo broke his leg at baseball—but not to worry—you would read my last chapter from your iPhone in the ER while you waited for the doctor. And two hours later you sent me terrific notes. Seriously, that was crazy and amazing, and I would name my first child after you if it weren't too late.

To my dad, the prolific novelist Paul Levine, thank you for editing every word of my book. It's a subject that couldn't be further from your own interests or demographic and yet you found greatness in every chapter. And I am incredibly grateful that you connected me to the venerable and dapper literary agent Al Zuckerman of Writers House. Thank you, Al, for believing in this book, believing in me, and reminding me regularly how fiery and sparkly I am. Nothing makes a forty-four-year-old woman smile more than hearing that she still sparkles.

I would not have had any perspective on my book if it weren't for my devoted readers: Nikki Kessler, Sharon Nevins, Jessica Spira, and my amazing sister Debra Feinberg. Thank you for your feedback, smarts, and unwavering support. A special shoutout to my bestie, my soul sister, my eternal "boast bitch" since seventh grade, Nikki Kessler, for always loving what I write and encouraging me in all I do. Thank you for dissecting my thesis and making sure what I wanted to say made sense. To Gayle Greenberger, whose story is not in this book but whose presence is greatly felt, your honesty and resilience is reflected in many of its themes. Thank you for twenty-five years of unconditional friendship. You are my judgment-free fly zone.

Meredith Sinclair, you make one of the mantras in this book, "I shine, when you shine," truly come to life, and you make a life well-played, well, possible. Karen Wolf, Debbie Otner, and Katie Fleetwood, I truly appreciate your checking in on my fragile mental state over the course of writing this book and for the celebratory dinners, cocktails, and ample wine. Lyss Stern, thank you for always connecting me to just the right people at just the right time. Barbara Messing, my two-time college roomie, exceptionally smart and devoted friend, thank you for all of your enthusiastic support and love for nearly three decades. Among my more random, but awesome gigs, I was an on-camera "travel expert" because of you.

Having had so many jobs, I'm fortunate for the incredible and lasting connections I've made to so many. In different ways, you have all buoyed and encouraged me throughout my multiple career pivots. To my *Dateline NBC* family, my *Dateline* gig remains, hands down, the best and most stressful job I ever had. Neal Shapiro, Marc Rosenwasser, Jamie Bright, Carolyn Goldman, Brad Davis, Heather Vincent, Jocelyn Cordova, Travis Rundlet, Marianne Haggerty, Julie Cohen, Stacey Reiss—and the list goes on. Neal, we all still worship you. To DKC, the most creative and innovative media and PR shop around, I am proud to call myself a veteran. Thank you, Matt Traub, Sean Cassidy, Adam Schiff, Rachel Carr, Joe DePlasco, and, of course, Jo Flattery. Frieda Orange, Emily Mailaender, and Alexandra Ezra, you were my awesome lady bonobos at Rubenstein. To the unflappable and brilliant Sheila Marcelo, Care.com's badass CEO and founder, you are an inspiration to all women.

ACKNOWLEDGMENTS

I am grateful to my editors Ellen Kadin and Barry Richardson and the incredible team at AMACOM. Thank you for your enthusiasm for my book and for seeing all of its potential.

So much of what inspires my writing comes from my experience in motherhood. I am forever thankful to my delightful, spirited, and intuitive daughter Lexi for asking me daily how my writing was going and reminding me that I was her role model, especially when I needed to hear it the most. In many ways, I write this book for you. And to my ridiculously creative, strategic, and tech-savvy son Jonah, who always has an eye on monetizing my content. I'm grateful that someone is always thinking about the bottom line. Thank you, Jonah, for redesigning my website and making sure that my social feeds are getting close to what they should be.

This book would never have been written without the total encouragement and love from my husband Michael. Always my number-one fan, he has cheered me on every step of the way—supporting every career pivot, epic fail, and relaunch. You have my heart.

And a final thank-you to Julie Pauly and the Able Baker in Maplewood, New Jersey, where I spent endless hours over many months squatting at my corner table writing this book. Thank you to Able Baker's barista Max Stone for the perfect lattes and to the morning coffee klatch who cheerfully asked me every day how the book was coming along. It's finally done!

Contents

CONTENTS

INTRODUCTION

IN AUGUST 2014, I LOST my freelancing job as the Director of Content at Grey, a global, hundred-year-old advertising agency, often referenced in *Mad Men*. It's where Duck Phillips landed after being dumped by Sterling Cooper. Because Grey slashed my short-lived position, a frequent mini-tragedy at ad agencies, I was searching for a new full-time gig. I became obsessed with joining one of the bright, shiny digital media start-ups in New York City, partly out of fear that if I didn't work at a hot tech-based company, I would soon become a dinosaur. I had studied journalism, and traditional media were on life support. As a Gen Xer, I felt my professional currency was quickly fading, and I needed to switch gears so I could sparkle...or at the very least find a job.

I interviewed at a small hybrid PR/social media agency where a dozen under-thirty-somethings sat shoulder-to-shoulder on ergonomic chairs, huddled around an eco-friendly reclaimed oak table. Macs lit up the room as an Irish Setter meandered down the narrow aisles looking to be scratched. In a makeshift meeting room, the bearded Millennial interviewing me studied my resumé on his laptop, refusing its paper version on ethical grounds. "We like to save trees around here," he said. I smiled and shoved my offensive wad of resumes and bios back into my bag. Old school, I invariably carry multiple hard copies to interviews.

"I see that you were a press secretary on Capitol Hill," he began.

"Yes!" I exclaimed, excited that the hipster noticed my first jobs out of college. While in my early twenties, I worked for two Democratic members of Congress during the Clinton administration, jobs that I always thought were impressive and important.

"Well, the way we operate here is that we have good relationships with the media," the Millennial sniffed. "Relationships are everything. It concerns me that you worked in politics. I mean I wouldn't want you slamming down the phone and pissing people off."

Huh?

Until now, my political experience had opened doors and given me a certain gravitas and credibility. The Hill was the Google of the Gen X generation, paving the way for big-time careers. After Capitol Hill, I worked at *Dateline NBC*, FOX, and CNN. I'd had a smorgasbord of interesting jobs, but this guy was put off by my political background from the mid-1990s. "I'm not a character in *Veep* or *House of Cards*," I said cheerfully. "I started as a twenty-one-year-old working for a freshman congressman from Miami in a super-crowded media market. I was begging reporters to cover us. I wasn't hanging up on anyone."

As I slunk out the door after grabbing a handful of kale chips and a coconut water, I realized that this struck at a bigger issue. I, a solid Gen Xer, who came of age during Walkmans and Diet Coke, was more culturally disconnected from this Millennial than I had imagined. Walking down Fifth Avenue, I realized my personal career pivot was going to be harder than I expected. I needed to hone my story. I needed to repackage my narrative and sell my skillset.

I needed to own my experience but reposition my pitch. I might even need to take a big pay cut and move backward before I could move forward again.

THE CURIOUS WORLD OF SILICON VALLEY

Big trends have a way of touching all of us. From tattoos to Birkenstocks to gay marriage, certain ideas, products, and political movements have an uncanny ability to reach critical mass and then gain acceptance, folding into the fabric of our collective culture. Today, Silicon Valley and the start-up world are our cultural crushes. It's part mythology with its unicorns, the billion-dollar start-ups like Uber and Airbnb, and part psychology with its change-the-world, disrupt-the-status quo, always innovating ethos. In the past decade, Silicon Valley has become our North Star, influencing everything from news and entertainment to public policy and workplace culture.

The celebrated start-up model of disruption that embraces failing fast and pivoting is not a typically female one. Women tend to be more risk averse. We can overthink our next move and not act until we're 100 percent ready.[1] We may feel like frauds when we're trying something new. Instead of being disruptive, women tend to be more disciplined. And we're often not pivoting—because we're stuck.[2]

So what if women embraced the start-up model? What if we had the confidence to take risks, even if we knew we might fail first? What if instead of agonizing about which step to take, we leapt forward quickly? What if we could apply lessons of iteration, engineering serendipity, failing fast, networking, and strategic branding to help us redirect our path, enhance ourselves, or transform our careers? No one has spoken to women in these terms yet, and it's not because we aren't wearing the requisite hacker hoodie. It's because we still have a Barbie problem.

BLAME IT ON BARBIE

Barbie knows something about career pivots. Since she debuted in 1959, she's had 150 different careers. Her eclectic resume ranges from swimsuit supermodel to President of the United States. But her entree into the tech world in 2014 was an epic fail. The Barbie controversy exploded, fittingly, in the blogosphere after author and Disney screenwriter Pamela Ribon read the children's book *Barbie: I Can Be a Computer Engineer*. In the book, Skipper asks if she can play the video game that she thinks Barbie is making. Barbie laughs and says that she's only creating the design ideas. "I'll need Steven and Brian's help to turn it into a real game!" Barbie doesn't know how to code, but she does know how to draw cute puppies. Barbie then gets a virus on her computer that infects Skipper's hard drive, causing Skipper to lose her homework and music files. Silly Barbie!

"'Hi, guys,' says Barbie. 'I tried to send you my designs, but I ended up crashing my laptop—and Skipper's, too! I need to get back the lost files and repair both of our laptops.'"

"'It will go faster if Brian and I help,'" offers Steven.

The boy programmers save the day and fix Skipper's hot pink laptop, but Barbie takes credit for their work. Outraged by the insulting story, screenwriter Ribon blogged about Barbie and the story went viral. Barbie haters were out in force and a call to action was posted on a Facebook page for people to rewrite the storyline. Kathleen Tuite, a computer engineer, created the Feminist Barbie Hacker site, seeking female programmers to help crowdsource new text for the book. Tuite got more than two thousand submissions. Mattel issued an apology and Random House pulled the book from Amazon.[3] This was more than just another bad PR day for Barbie. To many this was further proof that not only does the tech world have a massive girl problem, but also that culturally we still think we need the boys to fix our laptops.

As the tech industry reinvents how we work, where we work, and the kind of work we all do, it's important that women across all industries understand how to use the valuable lessons and themes from Silicon Valley for our own advancement. Whatever our career, we need to hack the code and rewrite our own storyline. All too often, we watch the guys do it. They iterate, pivot, and progress. Like Barbie's guy friends, they design the game and save the day, while women are left behind, drawing the puppies.

Studies show that women may not reach for the brass ring because, afraid we won't succeed, we won't even try. Inertia is a confidence killer, and with the world today moving at the speed of social, there is no time to get stuck.

AGILE AND RELEVANT

In the past dozen years, even as the economy has contracted and people have lost jobs, we've seen an explosion of entirely new industries. Some careers have completely disappeared while others have morphed or evolved. Job titles that didn't exist ten years ago—like social media manager, data scientist, and IOS developer—are flourishing.

"There is no such thing as a career path now," says Karen Shnek Lippman, a managing director at the Sloan-Koller Group, a recruiting firm in New York. "The only career goal you should be focusing on right now is staying relevant."[4]

On and off for the past twenty years, I've been pivoting so much it feels more like pirouetting. I started in politics, moved into TV news, and toggled back and forth in various strategic communications, content, and editorial jobs. I've worked at start-ups and legacy companies. And among my more random gigs, I appeared as the on-air spokesperson for TripAdvisor. I like to say that I'm not a travel expert, but I played one on TV.

To be clear, my professional pivoting wasn't always intentional. I didn't plan to tweak my career every few years; at first, it just happened. I got fired from jobs, I lost jobs when funding faded and start-ups folded, and I got pregnant twice. And certain careers—specifically those that require last-minute travel—aren't easily compatible with having small children. But in recent years, as the digital universe has blown up the media landscape, I tried to become more purposely strategic and entrepreneurial in managing my career.

LinkedIn's co founder Reid Hoffman says that these days everyone needs to think of himself or herself as an entrepreneur, even if you're not running your own business. What's important today, he writes in his book *The Start-Up of You,* is an entrepreneurial mindset. With that comes the ability to adapt and change things up, which is vital to succeeding in today's workforce.[5]

More than ever, employers today expect that people will learn on the job—and learn quickly. They also don't expect that you will stick around for too long. A recent study found that 91 percent of Millennials will stay in their jobs for less than three years and will have four jobs in their first decade out of college. Job hopping is the new normal, and agility is the must-have skill.[6]

"There are so many hybrid roles now that require someone with multiple skillsets," Shnek Lippman says. "You can't just be an editor anymore. You have to be an expert in audience development. You have to understand how mobile works. It's a wild carpet ride and you have to be ready to work in different function areas than you are used to, and embrace it with an open mind, because it's the only way to survive."

WE MUST LEARN HOW TO PIVOT

The good news is that in many industries there is no longer a linear path to professional success. Technology has disrupted fields including retail, media, marketing, sales, advertising, and even law, creating millions of new jobs and hacking that professional ladder in the process. The climb is more indirect. But having the courage and confidence to make the move and take risks is critical. And for women, the lack of boldness and how we perceive and position ourselves is what often holds us back.

Many of us don't fit neatly into the professional bento box. The benign question "So what do you do?" can set off a tsunami of existential angst.

"When I'm not working on a project, I feel like a fraud to say that I have a company," entertainment producer Nikki Kessler says. "So sometimes I wonder, am I retired? Am I a producer? Am I just a mom? What am I?"

This book is for women at all stages of their professional journeys. Some may be looking for a total relaunch. Others are trying to reposition themselves to stay relevant. Still more may be looking to get back into the game after taking time off to raise kids and need the confidence and direction to take the first step. The women in this book span generations, from Millennials to Baby Boomers. The majority are Gen Xers—those born between 1960 and 1980. The common thread is that everyone in the book has pivoted or relaunched themselves. Their stories show how risk-taking, moments of gumption, staying true to yourself, and even baby steps will move you forward.

In fact, even the space where I wrote this book, the Able Baker in South Orange, New Jersey, has its own relaunch story that began as many do—in misfortune. Bakery owner Julie Pauly lost her retail management job in New York City the day after Christmas in 2008, the year the economy tanked and Lehman Brothers went bankrupt. Unable to find a new job, Julie turned a passion for baking and a way to keep busy while unemployed into a thriving local business in suburban New Jersey. Julie's bakery and its decadent scones have been profiled in *The New York Times*.

As Madeleine Albright has famously said, women's careers are usually not linear; they zigzag. Women need to embrace the zigzag. To move forward we need the inner confidence to make a professional change and the outer confidence to make ourselves heard and noticed. We need to stop apologizing, afraid of offending, and instead be direct in voicing our opinions. We need to understand how to capitalize on our skills and give value to our experience—even the volunteer work. We need to craft a story, own our message, and develop networks to help amplify our voices. We need to create the momentum for change.

We are the generations of women who were raised in a culture to march forward. Now we must learn how to pivot.

1

CHANGE YOUR WORDS
Boost Your Brand

"Your time is now. Work on purpose and with purpose. Never get stuck. Pursue your passions. Make bold moves. Beware the status quo. Leave a gentle footprint."

—SWEETGREEN

'M STANDING FIFTY-PERSON DEEP IN a line snaking down the block at sweetgreen, a farm-to-table, on-the-go salad shop in the Flatiron area of New York City. The sweetgreen manifesto hangs prominently near the entrance, an inspirational beacon beckoning us into a fragrant store filled with organic kale and humanely raised, hormone-free roasted chicken. I come to sweetgreen and endure the wait not only because of the locally sourced produce, but also because of the vibe. There's something uplifting amidst the spicy sunflower seeds and baked falafel balls. The sustainability-meets-SoulCycle empowerment message resonates with me. "Our delicious and healthy food aligns with your values," reads the "Our Story" page on the sweetgreen website.

Today every brand, like every comic book superhero, has an origin story—from Warby Parker eyeglasses to TOMS shoes to the quinoa I'm consuming at sweetgreen. We women each have our stories too. We need to define them, own them, and sell them. Most of us aren't walking around with a personal manifesto tattooed on our backs, so how we present ourselves to the world, not only in person but also online, has tremendous impact. We know our LinkedIn profiles and curated social feeds represent what we stand for and care about. We may be cautious or even precious about what we post, wanting to craft a certain image. But there is another piece to how we outwardly present ourselves and control our message—and it's as obvious as it is subtle. The language we use in person and in email sets a tone, and in just a few words it can convey our confidence or our insecurity. What we think may be a friendly, conversational style can inadvertently be harming us. Without realizing it, we women sometimes sabotage ourselves, our brand identity, and our professional currency with small words and phrases that qualify what we say and diminish our power before we even begin.

OWN YOUR POWER: NEVER SAY SORRY

"Sorry." It's a word that my dear friend and former colleague Jo Flattery, forty-three, a smart, seasoned, incredibly likable PR maven in New York City, used to use a lot. It worked for her. "It can take the tension out of the room," Jo tells me as we sit eating our sweetgreen salads.

Jo has a warm, earthy vibe that is as disarming as it is honest. She is masterful at scoring major press hits but is equally astute at assuaging combustible egos. Jo's former boss would bring her to meetings with the tough clients because she is intuitively skilled at making alpha males a little softer and gentler. "I am the pony that cools down the horses. I am a Gemini and a middle child and am always looking to make the peace," Jo says smiling, dimples flashing.

Jo's style is unfiltered, but not brash. After years of listening to

Jo use "sorry" as a way to deflect seeming too forward, I started using it. It worked like a charm. It was a lovely social lubricant that made what I say silkier, softer—perhaps easier to digest. A few years earlier I had left a job at a start-up where my boss had told me I came off as too abrasive. Because I worked remotely in New York and the company was based in Boston, much of my communication with my colleagues was over the phone. "They just don't see the real you," my boss would tell me. "They don't know you like I do and see your smile or your body language." It was supposed to be professional constructive criticism, but it felt personal.

Feeling insecure about how I was being perceived at work, I began trying out Jo's "sorry." People never accused Jo of being bitchy or abrasive. Was it because she was blonde and petite? Or was it the language she used? Maybe it was a little of both. So I started apologizing.

I got a new gig at Grey advertising and took my "sorry approach" with me. I was working with a lot of young hotshot guys, and it easily slipped into my vernacular. No one seemed turned off or threatened by my direct approach or accused me of being bossy because, well, maybe I wasn't so direct anymore. My "sorry" became almost deferential: "Sorry, how do I share my plan with the team?" It became my way into conversation. "Sorry, can I ask you a question?" Ironically, a shampoo ad produced by Grey while I was working there immediately ended my apologizing. I was now suddenly sorry for using "sorry."

The Pantene ad that launched in 2014 shows how women use the apology as a subconscious technique to downplay power or to soften what they want to say. In the ad, we see women in different scenarios constantly apologizing. At work, a woman sitting in a conference room looks up and says to a man standing over her, "Can I ask a stupid question?" At home in the kitchen, a mom says "sorry" as she hands her baby over to a man who seems to be her husband. And "sorry" is used with strangers: A man bumps into a woman as he sits down next to her and stretches out. He knocks her knees but *she* apologizes. A woman gets into a car with a guy who appears to be her friend. They start talking at the same time, the woman says, "Sorry, you go first."[1]

The women apologize not for being rude or hurting someone, but for asking questions and simply taking up space. What I had thought was a breezy approach to engagement suddenly became loaded with lady baggage. "Sorry" isn't just an apology for a screw up, it's also a way to make sure you aren't accused of being bossy, bitchy, or too aggressive. It's filler; it's a crutch; it's a way to appear gentler when you are asking for something. It's a power deflator that sucks the energy away from what you are saying.

AMY SCHUMER IS NOT SORRY

Amy Schumer took on the "sorry" state of how women speak in a May 2015 sketch on her show *Inside Amy Schumer*, where she skewered our propensity to apologize. The scene is set at a "Females in Innovation" conference during a panel with top innovators in their fields, including Schumer as a scientist who studies neuropeptides. The other women on the panel are equally accomplished: There's a Nobel Prize winner, a Pulitzer Prize winner, a woman who invented a solar panel water filtration system, and a woman who built a school for child soldiers. The sketch opens with the panelists apologizing for correcting the male moderator as he introduces each of them incorrectly. He screws up, but the women apologize. Then they apologize for talking over each other. Pretty soon the sketch becomes more ridiculous, devolving into a scene of "sorrys."

"Sorry, I hated that."

"Sorry, I wish I hadn't said that."

"Sorry, is this coffee? Sorry, this is my fault."

At one point a stagehand delivers a cup of coffee to one of the panelists, who had clearly asked for water, saying she's allergic to caffeine. He delivers it anyway and, in the process, spills the coffee on another panelist. The woman writhes in pain on the floor, blood gushes from her legs, and *she* apologizes. The other women join in. It becomes an absurd symphony of "I'm sorrys," leaving the male moderator completely confused.[2]

DON'T DILUTE YOUR MESSAGE

Tami Reiss, CEO of tech company Cyrus Innovation, saw this sketch, as did many of the women with her at a brunch for the League of Extraordinary Women. They discussed how they fell into the habit of using these "shrinker" words even though they knew they shouldn't. They also spoke about an article that had recently run in *The Washington Post*, "Famous Quotes: The Way a Woman Would Have to Say Them in a Meeting." In this spoof, reporter Alexandra Petri gives iconic quotes the lady treatment.[3]

▶ "Give me liberty, or give me death."

Woman in a meeting: "Dave, if I could, I could just—I just really feel like if we had liberty it would be terrific, and the alternative would just be awful, you know? That's just how it strikes me. I don't know."

▶ "I have a dream today!"

Woman in a meeting: "I'm sorry, I just had this idea—it's probably crazy, but—look, just as long as we're throwing things out here—I had sort of an idea or vision about maybe the future?"

▶ "Let my people go."

Woman in a meeting: "Pharaoh, listen, I totally hear where you're coming from on this. I totally do. And I don't want to butt in if you've come to a decision here, but, just, I have to say, would you consider that an argument for maybe releasing these people could conceivably have merit? Or is that already off the table?"

Tami says the conversation about how women are not comfortable being direct is not new to her. At work events, including those that advised women on how to attract business investors, women had been encouraged not to undermine themselves and their businesses with words like "we think" and "we hope to." It was becoming all too obvious that something needed to be done—an effective means of alerting women that they were softening their language when instead they should be speaking directly and with confidence. What if there was something like a spell-check for "sorry," Tami suggested to a friend sitting next to her at a girlfriends' brunch. What if she were to make an online tool that would highlight those trigger words? The women at the brunch loved the idea. One even agreed to do some pro bono PR when it launched.

In December 2015, Tami released the "Just Not Sorry" Gmail plug-in that alerts you when you type certain words including "just," "actually," "sorry," "I think," and "I'm not an expert..." The plug-in underlines the words as you type. If you hover over the words, it explains how you may be undermining your confidence in your message.

"It's a mindfulness exercise," Tami says. "It makes you conscious of when to use the words and when not to use them. We designed this as an awareness exercise, and we knew it would take off with women."

What surprised Tami was that it took off with the press too. Within a day of its launch, everyone from BBC News and NPR to NBC's *Today* show was talking about "Just, Not Sorry" and calling Tami for interviews. It struck a nerve.

"This is a way of saying to women, you are consciously stepping in your own way," Tami says. "If your default is to say 'sorry' and use undermining words, by eliminating even half of them, you would be more respected."

BEYONCÉ: "SORRY, I AIN'T SORRY"

No doubt we are in the zeitgeist of "sorry," and if we needed any more confirmation of its popularity, we need to look no farther than our reigning culture queen, Beyoncé. In April 2016, Beyoncé released *Lemonade*, an album with song lyrics wrapped in innuendo that begged for examination. Had Jay-Z really cheated on Bey? Beyoncé's song "Sorry," with a literal chorus of "Sorry, I ain't sorry," seemed to be outing her husband's infidelity but making clear that as a fierce and independent woman, Queen Bey would never apologize.

The fiery song inspired Lena Dunham, the actress, writer, and director behind the TV show *Girls*, to discuss her near-pathological relationship with "sorry." Weeks after the *Lemonade* debut, on May 25, 2016, Lena Dunham posted a piece on LinkedIn titled "Sorry Not Sorry: My Apology Addiction":

> I am a woman who is sometimes right, sometimes wrong but somehow always sorry. And this has never been more clear to me than in the six years since I became a boss. It's hard for many of us to own our power, but as a 24-year-old woman (girl, gal, whatever I was) I felt an acute and dangerous mix of total confidence and the worst imposter

syndrome imaginable. I had men more than twice my age for whom I was the final word on the set of *Girls*, and I had to express my needs and desires clearly to a slew of lawyers, agents, and writers. And while my commitment to my work overrode almost any performance anxiety I had, it didn't override my hardwired instinct to apologize. If I changed my mind, if someone disagreed with me, even if someone else misheard me or made a mistake . . . I was so, so sorry.

Perhaps it's telling that Dunham, the Millennial emblem of modern-day feminism and unfiltered fearlessness, is also not immune to the instinct to apologize. It's a habit that plagues even the bravest among us.

PLAYING BIG

All of these "sorrys" do add up, says Tara Mohr, author of *Playing Big: Find Your Voice, Your Mission, Your Message*. Mohr, a career and personal growth coach, teaches women how to find their voices, ignore their inner critics, and carve out meaningful careers. "Sometimes we say we're sorry out of habit and it's unintentional, but sometimes we do it because we have a sense that we need to soften what we're saying or ensure that we come across as non threatening and as a nice girl," says Mohr. "We are acting out a double bind trying to straddle the middle to make sure we don't offend anyone."

Mohr says research shows we assess a person's warmth in a very quick and immediate way. It's the first thing we size up. We are feeling their vibe. Do we like them or not like them? But competence, on the other hand, is something we ascertain over time.

"It's an evolutionary concept. People are really assessing friend or foe," Mohr says. "We focus on warmth in that first interaction, and then when we are feeling that we like that person, there is more room to demonstrate competence. The key is how to communicate warmth without dumbing yourself down."

Mohr talks about using a bookending approach: Open and close in a warm and personal way in a meeting or over email.

"At the beginning of the meeting, take three to five minutes to chat about the weekend or pets or something to make that human connection, and then show your competence. But close with something warm and friendly to convey your emotional warmth and accessibility," Mohr says.

Navigating work emails, where the goal is to sound friendly but professional, is exactly where all of this can fall apart. Recognizing this, Jo Flattery has changed the way she's communicating online.

"It can be hard to make a personal connection over email," Jo says. "Plus, with the deadline-driven world of news and client management, I found myself apologizing a lot, often when I didn't do anything wrong. It was out of habit. At first I had used it to ease the tension, but then I found myself using it as a transition word. The real lightbulb moment came when I was working on a project and sent a group email to say 'Sorry, here's the situation' about something that I had nothing to do with and which, frankly, wasn't even awful.

"A man on the project, who became a good friend and mentor, called me right away and asked me why I was apologizing for something that didn't even have any merit. And he said, 'Never say you're sorry in an email. Don't create an electronic trail. If you screwed up, it doesn't matter. Just say, here's the situation.' After that, I became much more aware of how easily I would take the fall for something that had nothing to do with me or something that was just totally out of my hands. I stopped intentionally writing 'sorry,' although I find myself still having to delete the occasional 'sorrys' that slip in. When I have to apologize now, I do it in person or I'll pick up the phone. I don't do it over email."

Aside from "sorry," there are other little things that Mohr says minimize our language. Even the smallest words pack tremendous punch and effectively shut down our power. The disclaimers "just," "actually," and "almost" may soften our tone, but they crush our confidence. Mohr recommends scrutinizing your sentences and scrubbing your email for qualifier phrases like "I'm just thinking off the top of my head…" or "I'm no expert in this, but…" She says delete the qualifier and just say what you want to say. Also, check for instances of sentences or phrases like "Does this make sense?" and "Do you know what I mean?" You shouldn't imply that you are incoherent. Instead, you can say, "Let me know if you have any questions about this." You can close in a personable way at the end, just don't distract from what you are saying. When the intent of your email is straightforward and clear, you are more likely to get a response.

THE DOUBLE BIND: LIKABILITY VS. COMPETENCE

Much has been made about the double bind that women face. There is considerable research that explores the conundrum, including a 2007 Catalyst study, "The Double-Bind Dilemma for Women in Leadership: Damned If You Do, Doomed If You Don't."[4] The title says it all. Women are in a corner, and it's not the corner office. The study found that women in business are perceived as "too soft, too tough, and never just right." When women conform to gender stereotypes and appear nurturing, they are not viewed as strong leaders. But when women take on typically male leadership traits such as being assertive and direct, they are seen as too strident and not personable.

Deborah Tannen, a linguistics professor at Georgetown University and best-selling author who writes and lectures about gender and language, writes, "A double bind means you must obey two commands, but anything you do to fulfill one violates the other. While the requirements of a good leader and a good man are similar, the requirements of a good leader and a good woman are mutually exclusive. A good leader must be tough, but a good woman must not be. A good woman must be self-deprecating, but a good leader must not be."[5]

The double bind is the ultimate dilemma. It essentially shows that women who are likable are not perceived as competent and that women who perform well in their jobs are not well-liked. And likability goes a long way. Studies find that it's not the smartest person in the room who will always get the job—it's often the one people like the most. This became even more apparent during the 2016 Republican presidential primary, when language, gender, social norms, the double bind, and all that we thought we understood about the sanctity of presidential elections played out and exploded like never before.

The campaign seesawed from the absurd to the ugly, with Donald Trump, Marco Rubio, and Ted Cruz arguing over whose wife was hotter and whose penis was bigger—the bizarre and shocking locker-room banter reached extraordinary new lows, even for politics. It was a campaign where Donald Trump shamelessly called women dogs, pigs, and bimbos and ruthlessly degraded Fox News anchor Megyn Kelly for her looks, her skills, and her gender. He attacked his female political opponents too. "Look at the face—would anyone vote for that?" Trump said during an early Republican primary debate, mocking GOP presidential candidate Carly Fiorina, who was on stage with him at the time. At a rally a few months later, he told a crowd that Hillary Clinton "got schlonged" when Barack Obama beat her in 2008.[6]

Trump's toxic language not only insulted women, but it also offended Muslims, Hispanics, and African Americans. No one was spared, aside from Trump's base of working class white men. Trump was called unhinged, a demagogue, and a fascist, but while the media repeatedly took him to task for his hateful and misogynistic language, nothing stuck.[6] He made Ronald Reagan—the original Teflon President—look downright sticky.

Ironically (but not surprisingly), while Trump was posturing, inciting crowds, and throwing red meat to his supporters, it was Hillary Clinton who was perceived to be too shrill, too untrustworthy, and too inauthentic. She's the one who people—even women—said they didn't like.

No doubt, there will be Harvard Business School case studies about the 2016 election. As I write, I imagine entire university curricula are in the works dissecting and analyzing Trump's appeal. They won't only focus on how Trump tapped into the subtle or not so subtle racism and anger brewing in the country, they will also reflect on how masterful he was at playing and pandering to the public. It can be argued that no one but The Donald could ever get away with that kind of inflammatory public rhetoric and performance. But try to imagine a woman in Trump's leather Oxfords. Take away the toxic language and leave just his bluster and arrogance, and still there's no way that a woman could inhabit that persona—even a piece of it—and succeed. Not a chance.

IF YOU CAN'T FIGHT IT, OWN IT

No one personifies the double bind like Hillary Clinton. She is the torchbearer for the rest of us. In her tasteful pearls, pantsuits, and kitten heels, Hillary is the poster woman for the "damned if you do, doomed if you don't" dilemma. For the more than twenty-five years she's been in the public eye, Hillary has been shouldering the unfairness, double standards, and gender stereotypes of what a woman in leadership should or should not do. As First Lady in 1993, she was excoriated for taking on national health care—a massive policy move that was not part of the typical First Lady job description. She tried to pivot from the traditional First Lady role and expand her reach, but it was an epic fail for the entire Clinton administration. Americans weren't ready to see Hillary Clinton or any First Lady driving policy. They hadn't hired her to do that—in fact, they hadn't hired her at all. And it didn't matter to voters if Hillary had the chops to take it on; it was not her business to take it on.

Madame Pivoter

Hillary's defining moment came a couple years later in 1995 at the United Nations Conference on Women in Beijing, where she spoke about the abuse of women in China. The powerful words were unexpected from a First Lady: "If there is one message that echoes forth from this conference, let it be that human rights are women's rights and women's rights are human rights once and for all."[7] Now she had a platform she could own—it was authentic and linked back to her days in Arkansas and her experience fighting for women's issues.

And then five years later, in another first for a First Lady, Hillary ran and won public office, securing a U.S. Senate seat from New York. Even Hillary's advisers couldn't have imagined her running for office and running back to the lion's den of the Capitol after her husband's second term ended. After all, this is where a large swath of its members had spent the past eight years viciously attacking her and President Bill Clinton. As the first woman to be elected as a senator from New York, she was making all kinds of history—and after twenty-four years as a politician's wife, she was now a politician in her own right. For eight, years she served, enacted legislation, and by all accounts was a respected U.S. Senator.

In 2008, Hillary pivoted again, this time running unsuccessfully for President. She lost the Democratic nomination to Barack Obama but ultimately left her distinct mark—eighteen million marks, as she would say at her concession speech. "Although we weren't able to shatter that highest, hardest glass ceiling this time, thanks to you, it's got about eighteen million cracks in it. And the light is shining through like never before, filling us all with the hope and the sure knowledge that the path will be a little easier next time."[8]

The Hillz—A Social Media Sensation

In her next gig, serving in President Obama's Cabinet as Secretary of State from 2009 to 2013, Hillary emerged as an unlikely social media star. As she globetrotted, she became popular in the geek chic world of social media, even inspiring a meme—Hillz—after she was photographed checking her BlackBerry and wearing sunglasses aboard a military C-17 plane bound for Libya. The shot launched the Tumblr site Texts from Hillary Clinton, in which the Secretary sends snarky texts to everyone from actor Ryan Gosling to Facebook founder and CEO Mark Zuckerberg. She was the badass, wonky Secretary of State who had visited 112 countries and logged a whopping 956,000 miles.[9]

Skip ahead to the 2016 race. A seasoned veteran with more scar tissue, mileage, and experience than arguably any politician in modern history, and yet Hillary's campaign needed to reintroduce her to the electorate—as the friendly, warm, trustworthy grandma. The irony was not lost on Hillary; after all of these years, how could the voters still not know the real her? The campaign initially wanted to reimagine how Hillary was portrayed. They knew they were swimming upstream with many voters who just couldn't kick a certain image of Hillary—a complicated, tarnished image wrapped in scandals and controversies that had been baking for decades. So the campaign needed to do a massive makeover and roll out Hillary in all of her genuine, human awesomeness. But the narrative just never took. Instead, the sense that she was not likable, not trustworthy, not authentic, and couldn't connect persisted. What was dragging down Hillary's candidacy was subtle but pervasive.

So they decided to shift gears. If you can't fight it, own it. During the primaries, we saw Hillary finally reconcile the public's perception of her with humor. This time around, Hillary outed herself for not being a "natural politician." Despite two successful runs for the U.S. Senate and two more campaigns for President, Hillary ironically admitted the obvious—that she was uncomfortable campaigning and, unlike her husband, she was just not very good at it. In fact, her inability to connect on the public stage became a de facto campaign strategy: Parody your unlikability to make yourself more likable.

Jimmy Kimmel "Mansplains" to Hillary

Clinton took to late-night TV to roll out a more human Hillary. In one sketch on *Jimmy Kimmel Live!*, Jimmy "mansplains" to Hillary what she needs to do to get elected and he offers his help to make it happen. The sketch opens with Jimmy asking Hillary if she knows what "mansplaining" is.

Hillary answers, "Isn't it when men speak to women in a patronizing way?"

"Actually, it's when men speak to women in a condescending way, but you were close," Jimmy corrects her.

He asks Hillary to give a stump speech so he can critique her style and give her tips.

"Stop shouting," Jimmy says before she gets through her first line. "You come off as too shrill." Hillary overcorrects and Jimmy jumps in, "Speak up, we can't hear you. You're like a mouse up there; and you know what would be nice? If you smiled. Show some teeth! Oh my God, with the sour puss! Try to have some fun, this is like your dream—pretend like you're enjoying yourself!"

Hillary takes the advice and smiles, and then Jimmy scolds her. "Don't smile like that, it's too forced, it looks like you're faking it. Look happy. Just be careful with the face. You have to ask yourself, do I want to be President or do I want to be a Lakers girl?"

The sketch is a spoof of the impossible double bind and the scrutiny that Hillary so famously endures. Kimmel gives Hillary conflicting advice. She should be assertive but not too assertive. Happy but not too happy, otherwise she risks seeming disingenuous.

Finally, Hillary gets exasperated and says, "It's like nothing I do is right." And Jimmy agrees, "Yeah, you're not doing it right. I can't quite put my finger on it...It's something. It's that you're not..."

"A man," Hillary answers.

"Yes! That's it! You're not a man, but that was really cute the way you did it," Jimmy says.[10]

This sketch defined the primary season of the Hillary campaign. Her Democratic primary opponent Bernie Sanders, the socialist-leaning senator from Vermont, was beloved by the public and hardly scrutinized. No one made a fuss about his rumpled clothes, messy hair, or manic gestures on the podium. His homey-ness and "I-tell-it-like-it-is" vibe resonated, particularly with young people. Even though Sanders would make far-fetched policy promises that he couldn't possibly deliver, no one criticized his angry, finger-thrusting delivery. But Hillary got continuously critiqued—not for the content of her speeches, but for her *tone* of her voice during the speech.

THE XX DILEMMA

Robin Lakoff, author and professor Emerita of Linguistics at University of California, Berkeley, says we are conditioned to like politicians a certain way—and that way is very alpha male. The bombastic, confident, and finger-wagging style shows us who is in charge. It can be seen as exciting and even thrilling in its manliness.

"The tougher he is, the better we like him and the more we trust him. We call him 'authentic,' regardless of whether he is or not, or whatever we think that word means, because what we really mean by 'authentic' is 'fitting the expected stereotype,' Lakoff writes.[11]

Hillary couldn't compete with that. Her style is more cerebral than emotional. Beating her chest and pounding the podium to make a point would never fly—not just for Hillary, but for any woman. Lakoff has a revolutionary idea about what we Americans need to do to get over this whole double bind business when it comes to disrupting the natural bias we have against female leaders. She says it's on us to rethink how we listen to and evaluate women and to recondition what we think is "better" and even normal.[12]

Lakoff compares this to the stereotypes about women in professional sports in a pre-Title IX era. Female athletes were often dismissed for "playing like girls." They didn't have the same strength or ability or generate as much excitement as the guys. Their games weren't worthy of watching or financially supporting. Many would argue that this bias continues even decades after Title IX, but it is evolving. Serena Williams, U.S. Women's Soccer, and mixed martial artist Ronda Rousey have shown us that female talent is worth watching and is lucrative. We may still view women's sports through a slightly different lens than the way we watch the men's, and that's okay. Different, Lakoff says, is still good. Similarly, she argues that we need to reframe how women in leadership are assessed, and we need to learn new ways of listening and hearing women.

"The problem does not reside in Clinton's style, or in anything she does or does not do. It rests with us, her audience. We do not know how to listen to a woman speaking in public or private, but especially in public and most especially when seeking a symbolically powerful position. We, her audience, need to change our style—our style of listening and our habit of expectations. This is a lot to ask, but it is what we have to do for our country," writes Lakoff.[13]

Many women understand the double bind. You don't need Hillary Clinton's national presence to find yourself under a microscope and in a similarly uncomfortable position. Women leaders are held to the double standard of having to be competent *and* well-liked in order to "fit." Men are not expected to be likable and are not admonished if they aren't likable enough.

At that tech start-up where I worked, I felt like my personality was under scrutiny. I had always had an assertive manner, but there I was told I came off as abrasive. It was suggested that I be gentler and keep my head down. For years, I had worked the phones as an NBC booker and then as a producer convincing people to share their stories with me. I was also a public speaker and knew how to effectively communicate. Or at least I thought I did. I couldn't help but think that if I were a guy, the way I delivered my opinions wouldn't have been so scrutinized and I wouldn't have ruffled so many feathers. Of course there's no way to know this. Maybe they just really didn't like me, and my ovaries might have had nothing to do with it. But research shows there may be something more that's underlying how I was perceived.

Kieran Snyder writes in *Fortune* that there's a common perception at technology companies that women are much more likely to receive negative personality criticism than their male peers.

Snyder's study on employee reviews at twenty-eight companies confirmed this hunch. "Words like bossy, abrasive, strident and aggressive are used to describe women's behaviors when they lead; words like emotional and irrational describe their behaviors when they object."[14] Women are told to pipe down.

But this doesn't only happen in technology companies; it happens in Hollywood too.

GET OVER ADORABLE

Academy Award–winning actress Jennifer Lawrence wrote a much talked about essay in fellow actress/director Lena Dunham's feminist newsletter *Lenny Letter* in October 2015. Lawrence discussed not only the vast gender pay gap in Hollywood, but also her fear of speaking up and not being liked. Women, she wrote, are conditioned to keep quiet and play nice.

In her essay "Why Do I Make Less than My Male Co-Stars?" Jennifer Lawrence writes about the disparity between her salary and that of her *American Hustle* male co-stars. "When the Sony hack happened and I found out how much less I was being paid than the lucky people with dicks, I didn't get mad at Sony. I got mad at myself. I failed as a negotiator because I gave up early. I didn't want to keep fighting over millions of dollars that, frankly, due to two franchises, I don't need," she explains.

Like so many women, Lawrence didn't speak up because she wanted people to like her.

"I would be lying if I didn't say there was an element of wanting to be liked that influenced my decision to close the deal without a real fight. I didn't want to seem 'difficult' or 'spoiled,'" she confessed. "This is an element of my personality that I've been working against for years, and based on the statistics, I don't think I'm the only woman with this issue. Are we socially conditioned to behave this way?...Could there still be a lingering habit of trying to express our opinions in a certain way that doesn't 'offend' or 'scare' men?

"I'm over trying to find the 'adorable' way to state my opinion and still be likable! Fuck that," she concludes. "I don't think I've ever worked for a man in charge who spent time contemplating what angle he should use to have his voice heard. It's just heard.

"Again, this might have NOTHING to do with my vagina, but I wasn't completely wrong when another leaked Sony email revealed a producer referring to a fellow lead actress in a negotiation as a 'spoiled brat.'"[15]

BRATS, BITCHES, AND OTHER NAMES

Women don't want to be thought of as brats or bitches. But fear of speaking up can cause us to not speak up at all. After my job at the tech start-up, I started paying much more attention to my word choice. I decided to dial back my assertiveness. I started to hedge. I looked at other women—those nonaggressive types—and tried to mimic their tones. I didn't want to be viewed as aggressive or bossy, so for a few years I started to say "sorry." A lot. It worked beautifully. And then, like Jo Flattery, I stopped.

As women look for new job opportunities to pivot in our careers or to grow the ones we already have, we reach out for advice and guidance. We may be networking, cold calling, and emailing people who we hope can help us. But as we present ourselves to the world, we must not make the mistake of diminishing our personal brand with language that whittles our perceived confidence and reduces our power. As Beyoncé told *ELLE* magazine in an April 2016 interview about her business and launching her new clothing line Ivy Park, "Power is making things happen without asking for permission." And, one could add, without saying sorry.[16]

2

STRIKE A POSE AND
FEEL THE POWER

"The most common way people give up their power is by
thinking they don't have any."

— ALICE WALKER

EYONCÉ STRUTS ON STAGE, SWAGGER beaming off her
couture bejeweled bodysuit. A glittery halo of Girl Power
envelops her—it's so palpable you feel fierce just witnessing
it. In addition to our verbal language, our body language projects
another aura of confidence or lack of it. Queen Bey commands
attention even standing still—perhaps more so as she stands still.
Hands on hips, shoulders back, head tilted upwards, she occupies
space in a way that communicates confidence and authority. She is
a natural "Power Poser," and studies find that Beyoncé probably
feels pretty awesome standing this way too. It turns out that posture and presence have a boomerang effect. A strong pose makes
people feel powerful, and it has others see them as powerful.

Social psychologist Amy Cuddy, an associate professor at Harvard Business School, became an Internet sensation after her
2012 TED Talk on "Power Poses" and the Impostor Syndrome.
The Impostor Syndrome is that feeling of phoniness in people
who believe they are not intelligent, creative, or capable, despite

evidence of high achievement. With more than thirty million views, Cuddy's talk is the second most watched TED Talk in history. Cuddy's research found that when people make themselves physically big—stretching out, taking up space, putting hands on hips Wonder Woman style—they can raise their testosterone levels, lower anxiety, and temporarily elevate their confidence. Shockingly, your body language can affect your physiology.

The psychology of presence began to fascinate Cuddy when she came across research involving entrepreneurs pitching potential investors. The strongest predictor of who got the money was not connected to the substance of the pitch or the person's credentials, but rather who exhibited traits of "confidence, comfort level, and passionate enthusiasm." The findings were shocking. Did the research suggest that massive investment decisions were being made based solely on charisma?[1]

It turns out that traits like enthusiasm and self-assured confidence are crucial to who gets called back for a job interview and who ultimately gets the job. In fact, those candidates who don't convey those traits are widely considered less capable. With presence packing such a serious punch, Cuddy decided to dive into understanding the effects of how we present ourselves and how we can manipulate our personal presence. As she describes it, presence is not a permanent mode of being; it comes and goes from moment to moment. We can all tap into it and bring it when we need it. But first, we need to feel powerful. "Presence emerges when we feel personally powerful, which allows us to be acutely attuned to our most sincere selves," Cuddy writes.[2]

FAKE IT UNTIL YOU BECOME IT

Cuddy's personal story is as compelling as her research. She was a sophomore at the University of Colorado when a horrific car accident left her with a traumatic brain injury. Her doctors told her it was unlikely she would ever finish college or feel like herself again. Cuddy's IQ dropped thirty points. Nevertheless, she refused to accept that fate. She fought back, and after starting and stopping college a few times, she graduated, taking an additional four years to do so.

Cuddy went on to Princeton for graduate school, where she says she couldn't shake the idea that she didn't belong there—that it was a big mistake. Terrified to speak in public, Cuddy was prepared to quit school rather than give the requisite twenty-minute talk to her classmates. Cuddy's adviser assured her that she knew the material and explained all she needed to do was fake it. In other words, fake the confidence to show what you know and keep doing it until you own it. Cuddy's personal experience, together with what she saw in her students, inspired the research that ultimately became the famous TED Talk and the findings for her book, *Presence: Bringing Your Boldest Self to Your Biggest Challenges.*

The fake-it-until-you-make-it idea is not new, but Cuddy's findings that your posture can impact your confidence and therefore your ability to perform has taken the self-perception theory to a new level. If we want to see ourselves as creative, smart, and successful, then we need to behave that way, and part of that behavior is how we physically carry ourselves. Cuddy's mantra: fake it until you *become* it.

"It's not about deciding that you'll become the best tennis player in the world without ever having picked up a racquet. It's about how when we trick ourselves into feeling powerful by adopting these big postures, we can then reveal who we truly are. And the more we do this, the easier it becomes, and the more we become the best version of ourselves," Cuddy told NPR in an interview.[3]

Cuddy became intrigued with the power of posture on performance while watching her students at Harvard. Women, she observed, tended to shrink when asked questions, while the men shot their arms up and leaned forward. The women made themselves small, touched their necks and faces, and crossed their ankles. Clearly, these postures projected less confidence, but Cuddy wondered if they also impacted the way the women behaved in class. Could looking small cause the women to feel less confident and hamper their participation and performance in graduate school?

Cuddy decided to test the theory that making yourself physically bigger by using open expansive postures could affect hormone levels. She took saliva samples from the people she was testing before and after they struck their poses. The increase in testosterone was significant, as was the decrease in the stress hormone cortisol. Cuddy has done multiple studies confirming that "getting big" for two minutes raises testosterone and lowers cortisol levels in the brain, temporarily boosting confidence and lowering anxiety. She also found that the opposite postures—those small, wimpy ones—had the reverse effect: They caused cortisol to rise and testosterone to fall. Cuddy writes in *Presence* that big, expansive, take-up-space poses create the perfect hormonal profile for being on your A-game and drawing out your best. They create the ideal cocktail of assertiveness with low anxiety.

The stresses of the workplace, from job interviews and important meetings and pitches to performance evaluations, can put people into a primitive fight-or-flight state. These stressful situations can cause great anxiety, making some of us shut down or not perform well. But Cuddy argues that by adopting expansive positions, we can trick our brain into believing what our body is doing so we can better handle those stressful moments. "We are allowing our bodies to tell our minds that you are not in a threatening situation. You can rest and digest," she says.[4]

POWER POSING: CHANNEL YOUR INNER WONDER WOMAN

Confidence is rooted in the animal kingdom and wired into our biology. Among apes, the dominant males are the ones who throw their arms up in the air and literally take a stand. In the human world, the position of confidence is arms on hips, legs spread Wonder Woman style. And then there is the classic alpha male I-run-this-place pose, arms folded behind the head with legs kicked up on the desk. Think President Obama in the Oval Office. The other "power pose" is what Cuddy calls the "starfish"—arms thrown up in a "V" as the sprinter crosses the finish line of a race. Interestingly, researchers have found that the starfish pose, arms up wide in the air, is a universal sign of pride and confidence and actually hardwired into us. Even congenitally blind people use that gesture when they win.[5]

At the June 2015 G7 Summit in Bavaria, a photo of German Chancellor Angela Merkel and President Obama went viral. The image was of Merkel with snowcapped mountains behind her, arms open wide facing Obama as he stretched out on a bench facing her. His arms were draped out across the bench and his legs were wide open. Even if Obama tried, he couldn't get any bigger. The image was spoofed and Photoshopped, making Merkel appear as though she were Julie Andrews in *The Sound of Music*, singing with her arms outstretched and the picturesque mountains in the background. When the image made the rounds on social media, I was struck by how physically large both of these world leaders appeared. They were power posing without even posing. At the G7 Summit, a conference of the most powerful nations in the world, it's not surprising that both of these world leaders demonstrated confident body language. These postures are as natural to them as breathing. The G7 Summit image spoke volumes in a context where image is everything.[6]

After watching Amy's TED Talk on poses, I wanted to give it a try before my next job interview. Since interviewing for my first job on Capitol Hill, I have had my own pre-game performance rituals. Before I interview or give a speech, I go into a bathroom and have a pep talk with myself in front of the mirror. I also make sure there's nothing in my teeth. But this time, I decided I was going to channel Wonder Woman.

A few weeks later, I was up for a senior vice president position at a well-known New York City public relations agency. I put the timer on my iPhone for two minutes and stood in front of a bathroom stall, chatting silently to myself as I struck my Lynda Carter pose. My interview went smoothly, and after four callbacks (each time prepping with my Wonder Woman stance) I was offered the job. Did this power pose affect my ability to interview well? Perhaps. I was keenly aware of my posture during each interview. When I interview, I tend to lean in to show enthusiasm and interest. This time, as I did that, I tried to make myself a little bigger in the chair too, not Obama big with legs spread open, but bigger than my slight self. Who's to know if that impacted my performance or the aura I projected, but it felt good.

STAND OUT FROM THE CROWD

When Heidi Davis walks into a room, you notice. At nearly five feet ten inches tall, she carries herself like she's six foot two, which she often is because of the heels she favors. Being the tallest person in the room is largely genetics, but in Heidi's case it's also intentional. "I'm not comfortable *not* being the tallest person—I like being the tallest person always," Heidi says matter-of-factly. Hence, her high heels.

In many ways, Heidi's height defines her. It epitomizes her spirit, a bold, fierce, balls-to-the-walls type of energy and crisp confidence. Growing up in Marblehead, Massachusetts, with a head of kinky curls in a pre-Keratin era and taller than all the other girls, Heidi was described as "interesting looking," rarely pretty. "You can't buy height. I didn't get blonde hair and I didn't get blue eyes. I didn't get everybody else's look. So it's either embrace it or don't."

Heidi has always been tall, but she didn't always project confidence. It started blooming at Ithaca College, where she was eager to reinvent herself. At Ithaca, no one knew that in high school she had cleaned offices at night with her father so their family could eat something other than pizza or mac-and-cheese for dinner. No one knew that her family went bankrupt after her dad's deli failed, moved to Florida, and moved back to Massachusetts all within a year. No one knew that she never had a high school boyfriend or that she would be the first person in her family to graduate from college. Ithaca would be Heidi's fresh start. There she felt she could be anyone she wanted to be.

In October of Heidi's freshman year, her dad died suddenly of a heart attack. He was forty-four years old. The devastating loss took its toll on Heidi. She flunked her first semester and thought about quitting. But giving up is not in Heidi's DNA. She went back to school and became known around campus as much for her determination as for her height. Fully inhabiting her identity, she stood out and blossomed. Heidi was also always hustling, and in college she worked at the local lingerie store, Isadora.

"I think a lot of my drive comes because I had to. I came from a town where I was the Jewish girl in the J.Crew catalogue with my curly hair, no hair products, amid all of these Yankee girls and their sailboats. I always wanted something," Heidi says. "If I wanted it, I needed to get it myself."

Going After Her Dream

On the first day of her sophomore year, Heidi met Seth Davis, a smart guy with a wry wit and crates of bootleg Grateful Dead tapes. His five foot six stature never fazed Heidi. They clicked. They got each other. They were inseparable, and eventually they married. Just like a classic John Hughes rom-com where the ballsy girl from humble beginnings finds love and goes after her dream, Heidi packed up a truck and drove to New York City to start her life after graduation. It was December 1991, a week before Christmas, when Heidi, sporting suede shorts and a matching button-down fringe jacket, knocked on the door of the Hanky Panky lingerie office in the Garment District of New York. She introduced herself to the owner as the Heidi from Ithaca who would order the thong underwear for the Isadora store. They immediately hired her as the receptionist. In the elevator, Heidi did a little dance. She was pumped. Making $16,900 a year was going to be brutal in New York, but it was her first step.

After about a year at Hanky Panky, Heidi moved to another company in the Garment District and later landed at a job in the Times Two showroom. This put her on the path to becoming a fixture in the fashion world of Seventh Avenue. Heidi's plan was to own her own business by the time she was thirty years old. Now married to Seth, Heidi borrowed $20,000 from her in-laws and brought in a friend and former colleague as her partner. They took over a lease on West Thirty-Ninth Street in the Garment District and opened Hotline Showroom. Heidi had fulfilled her dream. At thirty years old, she was her own boss, building a company and a team of salespeople around the world. Within a year, she had repaid the $20,000 loan and had started collaborating with Joe Dahan, a hot emerging fashion designer from Los Angeles. He was designing T-shirts and dresses that would ultimately become the trendy brand Joe's Jeans.

For a decade, Heidi ran Hotline Showroom, until one day when her partner walked in and announced she wanted to buy Heidi out of their business. It wasn't friendly; it was a takeover. Her partner wanted lawyers, not mediation, and within weeks it was over. A fast divorce. Heidi had a deal, said goodbye to her employees, and walked out the door. While she felt some relief, she went through the many stages of grief. "At first, I felt woohoo, I'm free of almost ten thousand square feet of leases in Manhattan. I'm free of a six-figure line of credit. I'm free of a million-dollar payroll. But now where do I go? What do I do? I started this before I had children. Now I have children, but I'm not doing the PTA," Heidi tells me, her eyes tearing up.

The showroom had been her dream. She birthed it before she birthed her two children and grew it into a big business. Heidi, who has watched Amy Cuddy's famous TED Talk, says she can relate to that loss of self that Cuddy describes after a car accident left her with a traumatic brain injury. "Like Amy Cuddy says, she lost points on her IQ and that was her identity. She was the smart girl." Heidi says. "And I created fashion. I created trends. I created designer denim. I did that."

Heidi didn't want to drop out of the fashion industry, so she launched her own T-shirt line, Wash + Fold. But even after getting her T-shirts into Bloomingdales, after about a year she pulled the plug. It wasn't growing fast enough.

Slow Down, Then Reboot

Not knowing exactly what to do next, Heidi thought maybe she should take a break. It was good timing because her youngest child needed more of her attention. She started playing tennis, fully embracing the suburban mom cliché. She joined a tennis team. She became active in her kids' school but hated it. Ultimately, the uber-competitive doubles tennis culture with its full-time tennis regimen didn't sit well with Heidi. It became an unhealthy experience, one she described as akin to an addiction or an obsession. "You're enrolled. You travel. You take lessons. You buy a wardrobe for it. It's a full-on commitment," Heidi says. "And the women live for the affection from their pros."

Heidi started toying with the idea of becoming a realtor. She loved to renovate, and she loved the fashion and style of homes. Heidi saw that her skillset in style, fashion, and sales transferred seamlessly into real estate. The bar to entry is relatively low; getting a real estate license can be done fairly quickly. Heidi studied for her license and within a couple of months she was an agent with a job.

She pivoted from selling clothes to selling homes. Seth, always Heidi's biggest fan, told her she would kill it at real estate. He was right. The average realtor in New Jersey sold two houses in 2015. Heidi sold eleven.

Sell Yourself

"Welcome to my office," Heidi says to me as I slip into the front seat of her SUV. It's a day when agents view what's on the market, and I'm along for the ride. The first stop is a $400,000 home in a gentrifying middle-class neighborhood in Maplewood, New Jersey, that has recently flipped. Heidi jumps out of the car and talks at length to the Haitian contractor who owns the home and is hanging around outside. He's hustling too and wants to sell his property fast. Heidi matches the contractor's energy, speaks purposely, and takes his card. Flipping homes is the next business Heidi is considering. And yes, she tells this guy, she thinks his property will move quickly. I have no idea if Heidi really believes it will, but she's so self-assured in her delivery no one would doubt her.

Then we're off to a $3.9 million property in Short Hills, New Jersey. When we tour the homes, you must cover your shoes.

"Look at the ugly surgical shoe covers they put out for a $4 million home," Heidi says incredulously. "I bought slippers at Ikea for people to put on when they walk through my houses. These are the things that I do differently."

It's the details that make a difference. The tacky blue surgical slip-on shoe covers would never fly for Heidi. She puts out Fiji water and homemade guacamole. She helps owners stage their homes with the right furniture, flowers, and plants. She will move a ceramic vase or bowl to show off a counter. She will buy the proper pillows to give a facelift to a sofa. She'll play music and open doors, just so. This is where Heidi's creativity and skillset in fashion and business come together. This is where her career pivot shows just how much of her background she can bring to something new. And as an effective salesperson, Heidi's dogged persistence may be precisely how her mojo manifests best.

For realtors, strong relationships with builders are the Holy Grail. Heidi had her eyes set on one builder and his historic house in Short Hills. Heidi called and texted the builder at five thirty in the morning—when she got up to ride her bike—almost every day for a year, just checking in to see when he might be ready to sell. He finally called back. They met in person, and Heidi snagged the $4 million listing—an unusual feat for a newbie realtor, but it didn't surprise her. Heidi sees how her former sales experience folds perfectly into what she's currently doing in real estate. She has big plans for using blogs, podcasts, and social media in ways that the old-school brokers don't think about. "I'm not a realtor, I'm a salesperson," Heidi says. "It satisfies my sales energy, and it satisfies my creative energy."

Heidi's big presence is the fabric of her being. Many women don't carry themselves with the same level of overt confidence. As I walk through the homes with Heidi and then spend another day watching her interact with prospective buyers and other agents, it becomes obvious that Heidi *can* sell anything. She presents with such confidence that I would buy the property in the up-and-coming neighborhood or splurge on the multi-million manse if I could afford it, just because Heidi told me to. I ask Heidi how she thinks her posture and how she carries herself in the world impacts her business success from her Seventh Avenue days to selling real estate. She's never really thought about it. "I work on my forehand because that's not natural to me, but being confident is natural to me. Standing up tall is natural to me, and when someone says no, and I can turn it to the yes. That comes easily to me," Heidi says. "In my work now, I'm able to see the positives of a place—not because I've been a realtor for the past year and a half, but because I've been a professional salesperson since I was twenty-one. When the realtors I work with are learning their scripts and dialogues, it's like I'm at the US Open of that—I got that. That's the easy thing for me."

Turns out Beyoncé and Heidi may have something more in common than their posture. For Destiny's Child's first album cover, Beyoncé and the four other women are wearing black dresses from Follies, a designer Heidi had discovered and represented. And like Beyoncé, who uses her art as her voice (and as often is the case, has a voice because of her art), Heidi too is never shy of saying what she feels. "I always have to be heard," Heidi says. "I always have an opinion, and I often think I have a better way to do it. But that's part of my confidence."

HARDWIRED FOR CONFIDENCE

Many of us may think of confidence as a state of mind—an optimistic "can do" attitude. Some people like Heidi seem to brim with confidence, while others of us don't. We may also suspect that when it comes to confidence, men in general appear to have more of it. Deeply curious about the elusive nature of this seemingly intangible quality and wondering how gender impacts it all, journalists Katty Kay and Claire Shipman set out to explore female confidence in their best-selling book *The Confidence Code: The Science and Art of Self-Assurance—What Women Should Know.* Their research was shocking and disturbing. They discovered that we apparently are either hardwired for confidence or we're not. Like blue eyes, this inheritable trait is something we are born with—imprinted in our genetic code. Kay and Shipman found that the correlation between genes and confidence may be as high as 50 percent and may be even more closely connected than the link between genes and IQ.[7] Through their research they also discovered something that supports what Amy Cuddy saw earlier—that "success correlates more closely with confidence than it does with competence."[8] It turns out that when it comes to getting ahead, confidence *is* more important than ability.

In their book, Kay and Shipman write about Robert Plomin, a behavioral geneticist at King's College in Britain. Plomin, an expert in studying twins, has examined everything from intelligence to disease. Recently, he measured confidence in twins at ages seven and nine. The children were given standard IQ tests and tested in math, science, and writing. The children were asked to rate how confident they were about their abilities in each subject. Plomin found that the student's self-perceived ability rating (SPA) was a better predictor of achievement than IQ. The researchers also separated the fraternal twins from the identical ones and found the scores of identical twins were more closely related. These findings show how closely tied genetics are to our innate level of confidence.[9]

Cameron Anderson, a psychologist in the business school at the University of California, Berkeley, also studies confidence. In 2009, he conducted tests among his students analyzing the importance of confidence compared to competence, and how the students perceived each other within the group. Did confidence affect rank in the social hierarchy? Anderson concluded that confidence *does* matter more than competence. "When people are confident, when they think they are good at something, regardless of how good they actually are, they display a lot of nonverbal and verbal behavior," Anderson explained. From body language to a lower vocal tone to speaking in a calm and relaxed manner, he says confident people do a lot of things that make them look very adept in the eyes of others. "Whether they are good or not is kind of irrelevant."[10] And apparently all of this overconfidence is not a turnoff to others. In fact, Anderson found that the most confident people in the group were the "most beloved" and admired. The key here is that those with overconfidence weren't *faking it*—it wasn't simply bravado or bluster—they actually *believed* they were that good. When the level of confidence is authentic it fosters respect.[11]

This finding may be frustrating and troubling, but sadly it tells us something that many women in the workforce already know. Why is it that some people seem to always get the promotion or the better project or the job, even if they don't seem smarter or more qualified? I have experienced this firsthand—wondering why a guy was chosen over me. Did he just know how to "manage up" better? Was he going out for drinks after work with the boss? Did he have better chemistry with someone important? Or did he just come off as more capable because he appeared more confident?

The Gender Divide is Real

A growing body of research in recent years points to a true gender divide when it comes to confidence. Studies find that men overestimate their abilities and performance, while women underestimate both. This happens even when women perform equally well as (if not better than) men. Yes, guys can also feel insecure and self-doubt, but interestingly it doesn't stop them from moving ahead as frequently as it does women.[12] The gender disparity in salary negotiations is also well documented. Among business school students, studies have found men were asking for raises four times more frequently than women and were negotiating for 20 to 30 percent more.

Kay and Shipman dug deep into what it is that holds women back. Is a female brain wired differently from a male brain, therefore impacting confidence? It's a radioactive subject to suggest that women's brains somehow differ from men's. Historically, this is one of the issues that penalized women, a myth that women's minds were inferior to men's. But, in fact, men and women do have different ways of processing information. The majority of women's brain cell matter is located in the frontal cortex (the hub of reasoning) and in the limbic cortex (the emotional headquarters of the brain). Men's brain matter is distributed more evenly throughout the brain. Scientists also know that women's brains are more active than male brains in almost all areas, particularly the regions responsible for empathy, intuition, collaboration, and yes, even worry. But a byproduct of all of this emotional strength is our inability to turn off thoughts. We ruminate. We obsess. We can jump to conclusions.

"We think too much and think about the wrong things," write Kay and Shipman. "We are more keenly aware of everything happening around us, and that all becomes part of our cognitive stew. Ruminating drains the confidence from us."[13] Overthinking is debilitating. We might believe that we are problem solving, but instead our brains can start spinning out of control, interfering with our instincts and preventing us from moving forward. It becomes a vicious cycle: If we don't feel confident, we don't project competence and we become paralyzed.

Reframe and Stop Ruminating

There are tricks to end the rumination so we can take healthy action. Research shows we have to recognize the debilitating thoughts we are having and then give them an explanation—and it doesn't even have to be a reasonable one. For example, many of us feel if a phone call or email isn't returned quickly, then maybe that person doesn't like us or our work. Or maybe somehow we offended them, or worse, they want to fire us. But having even a ridiculous explanation for why you haven't heard back— like maybe the person you emailed broke their hand and can't type—suddenly reframes the situation and as Shipman says, "It gets you off the high speed train to darkness. It lets you step back again and become an observer of your thoughts and it's easier to say, 'I'm moving on. I'll email again in another two days, but I will stop putting all of this negative energy into it.'"

Shipman says that men simply don't agonize over these thoughts the way women do. They are better able to separate and externalize why an email or call didn't get returned. In fact, they are better equipped to process many situations that involve their personality, skills, and abilities. There has been extensive research on the gender differences in how students perceive their academic competence. Stanford psychology professor Dr. Carol Dweck famously found that when middle school boys did badly on a math test, they blamed the test for being too hard, but the girls blamed themselves for being bad at math.[14] The boys externalize. The girls, on the other hand, internalize and believe they are at fault. Other subsequent studies among older students and even adults yielded similar results. Women will fall on their sword, assuming they are somehow personally responsible, while men will find external circumstances rather than themselves to blame.

Rewire Your Brain to Become More Confident

While confidence may be partly genetic, the good news is that it is also very malleable. It's like a muscle that can be strengthened, or, with Amy Cuddy's "power posing," fooled. We can stand big, wide, and tall for two minutes to bring on confidence when we need it. We can also rewire our brains, even as adults. When we scrub those mental habits that hold us back and change our thinking, the science shows us there are physical changes in our brains as well. "You may be born with a propensity for confidence but it's something you build, and the root of confidence and confidence creation is very active. It's about taking action," Shipman says.

Confidence creation is about taking risks. There is no specific formula because we each have different concepts of what's risky. For some, it may be speaking in public. For others, it's negotiating a salary or applying for a job that maybe they feel underqualified for or don't have the specific experience for. For others, it's going out on their own and launching a business. But the root to building confidence is to challenge yourself, taking on whatever may be risky for *you*. "The key is getting yourself into a mindset every day where you are examining what your brain is telling you," Shipman says. "Can I push that? Can I try that? And why don't I just do that and move on?"

Other techniques that can rewire the brain to generate thought patterns that encourage confidence include cognitive behavioral therapy and meditation. Both have been found to be incredibly beneficial in calming the brain and stimulating confidence. When you meditate, the brain's fear center, the amygdala, shrinks and you can think clearly, which is obviously important for achieving goals.

When in Doubt, Act—Even if You're Afraid

Make no mistake—inertia kills confidence. Studies find that the most effective way to push back against self-doubt is to act. "Nothing builds confidence like taking action, especially when the action involves risk and failure," write Kay and Shipman.[15] Small steps (baby steps even) are essential to becoming confident—and confidence begets confidence. There is a snowball effect; the more you put out there, the stronger you will feel. "Having confidence propels us to take action, and the more we take action the more confidence we build," Shipman says. "It's a virtuous cycle."

But this may be easier said than done. Taking a risk and a leap will always require something to get you there. And what that something is can differ from person to person. Some suggest to "do it afraid"—acknowledge that yes, I'm scared and I'm going to do it anyway. You're owning your fear and being authentic about how you feel. The flip side of "doing it afraid" is what Cuddy discusses as "faking it until you become it." Shipman says you should do whatever it takes to get over that first hump. "In some ways we are all saying the same thing," she says. "Sometimes we need a crutch in order to take the first step that starts the process of creating the ability to take more action." And action is everything.

Don't Worry About Perfect

"Fail fast" is a mantra often heard in the tech industry. It's been embraced as the ultimate business model, and for founders who fail—at least for the guys in the hoodies—it's a notch in the belt and an essential part of risk-taking. The concept is that you push out a bunch of different prototypes or ideas and see what sticks, ignoring the rest. The expectation is that nothing that you first launch is perfect. It doesn't need to be. There's no time for perfection.

The quest for perfection is often what can keep women from getting ahead. "I think this 'perfectionist gene' that too many young women have holds them back, and instead they should really be aiming for 'good enough,'" Hillary Clinton told *Glamour* magazine. "You *don't* have to be perfect. Most men never think like that. They're just trying to figure out what's the opening and how they can seize it."[16]

An often-cited internal report from Hewlett-Packard shows the importance of confidence for women in the workplace. It found that women only apply for open jobs if they think they meet 100 percent of the criteria listed. Men apply if they meet 60 percent of the requirements. Sheryl Sandberg writes in her book *Lean In* that women need to shift from thinking "I'm not ready to do that" to thinking "I want to do that and I'll learn by doing it."[17]

The hinge to any type of career pivot is taking action—having the confidence and courage to try something new. All of this may explain someone like Heidi Davis. She may have won the genetic lottery on confidence; it may be imprinted into her DNA just like her curly hair. And perhaps because Heidi tends to naturally stand like Wonder Woman, the cocktail of power hormones may surge through her more frequently than the rest of us, giving her an extra boost. But Heidi also benefits from the byproduct of confidence. She believes and projects that she can succeed, which we now know helps her to succeed. Even in a major career pivot, from selling T-shirts to selling $4 million real estate, Heidi doesn't ruminate about what she doesn't know. She leans on her strengths and her skillset and goes all in.

"I always think, I've got to go for it myself," Heidi says. "I never think I don't belong here. Instead, it's yeah, I belong here! When I started in the Garment Center, I just did it. I brought results. I made it happen and it came back to me."

3

CREATE YOUR OWN
SERENDIPITY

"Difficult to see. Always in motion is the future."

—YODA

FOR AS LONG AS I'VE known Michael Salort, nearly twenty years now, he has been one of those lucky guys, professionally speaking. I'm not talking about the winning-the-IPO-lottery kind of luck. It's more like amazing things are constantly happening to him. His career cosmos always aligns, which by the way has benefitted me too—he has hired me three times.

Michael, who favors baseball hats and T-shirts and still has the boyish looks and helmet of hair of the TV news reporter he once was, has pivoted more times in his career than even he can remember. He also has an enviable network of contacts who inevitably seem to resurface years later, leading him to new opportunities. Since first working with Michael as an associate producer nearly two decades ago at the tabloid pseudo-news show *A New Current Affair* on FOX, I've always imagined Michael as the king of serendipity.

Michael's career began as a local TV reporter while he was still in college in Binghamton, New York. He moved through the local news circuit until he landed a bigger on-air gig at CNBC and later at FOX. He then switched to the producing side for ABC's *20/20*. Those jobs fit the trajectory of a journalist. But then in 2000, Michael pivoted into technology, working for Oracle CEO Larry Ellison's start-up, the New Internet Computer Company (NIC). Michael landed this gig through his colleague Gina Smith, ABC News's technology correspondent who was leaving ABC to run NIC and hired Michael to lead its business development and media. Michael hired me too.

Michael, who also had a side passion for writing, wrote a screenplay while working at NIC based on a story he had produced at *20/20*. He entered the screenplay in a contest and won, which led him to introductions and ultimately relationships with Hollywood producers. NIC imploded about two years after it launched, but Michael had now positioned himself as a technology executive who understood business development, fundraising, sales, and the start-up world. I, on the other hand, collected unemployment and had a baby. But as colorful career tales go, Michael's got even more surprising when he was recruited to run the digital arm of supermodel and TV host Tyra Banks's entertainment company, Bankable Enterprises.

Michael had landed the perfect job for himself. It combined all that he loved, from production to technology. Things continued to get interesting for him. As Michael was evaluating different ideas to grow the Tyra empire, he found a folder in the office called *Modelland*—a young adult book concept that had been scribbled down on the back of some napkins. Unlike the other ideas Tyra's team was considering, from branding candy to launching a talent management business, this was something that Michael was into. In fact, he was so into the concept that he offered to write the treatment for *Modelland* himself. Tyra was thrilled. The idea had been percolating for years, but no one was pushing it through. Within a week of finishing the book proposal, the idea was sold to Random House with Michael ultimately signing on to write the young adult fantasy novel about girls, friendships, and a wacky school where beautiful girls do crazy things. *Modelland* was published in 2011 and became a *New York Times* best seller.

Five years and a dozen projects later, Michael is currently writing a fictional memoir about a transgender married man, told from the wife's perspective. He was paid a six-figure advance from the man's wife, whom he had met through Gina Smith, the former ABC tech reporter who had hired Michael at NIC seventeen years earlier. Talk about coming full circle. And that's Michael's secret sauce. He nurtures his networks and stays top of mind. People remember him because he makes sure he's not forgotten.

As Michael's friend, I've been impressed, inspired, and even envious of his extraordinary career pivots. I've marveled at his ability to seamlessly expand his professional identity and get paid well for what he loves to do. There's no question that Michael is incredibly talented, charming, and agile. Married and the father of three, he has a full personal life too. So how does he do it? Is this a gender thing? Or is there a recipe for making this happen?

ENGINEERING SERENDIPITY

It turns out that Michael may be the king of serendipity but not in the way I had always thought. To understand what seems like Michael's magnificent good fortune, we need to take a closer look at what serendipity is all about.

As trends go, serendipity has become fashionable in Silicon Valley. At the annual South by Southwest (SXSW) Interactive Conference in Austin in 2013, thirty thousand techies, designers, creators, investors, and entrepreneurs met to discuss tech trends and best-in-class philosophies for start-ups and innovation. Several panels focused on serendipity and the importance of unexpected connections. While most of us think about serendipity as a "happy accident," the word's origin is more nuanced. It comes from a Persian fairy tale where three princes of Serendip "were always making discoveries, by accidents and sagacity, of things which they were not in quest of." This fairy tale, discussed in a now much quoted letter written in 1754 by British aristocrat Horace Walpole, has suddenly become legend in Silicon Valley.[1]

The entrepreneurial and creative classes are particularly enamored with this concept because of their understanding that the history of innovation and discovery can be traced to certain predictable situations. Steven Johnson, TED speaker and bestselling author of *Where Good Ideas Come From: The Natural History of Innovation,* has found systems in place that make it possible for great things to occur. Johnson says that it is almost never the lone researcher, scientist, coder, philosopher, artist, or academic who suddenly has that transformative lightbulb moment. Those are the stories that make for good tales. But the reality of an idea's genesis nearly always runs deeper. Johnson argues that the image of a scientist in a lab having a eureka moment is simply a myth. It turns out that the mash-up of creative collisions mixed with a little chaos, good timing, and human networks can spark the perfect storm for amazing ideas to take off. Engineering that perfect ecosystem to make incredible things happen is the obsession of the tech world. Simply, everyone wants the recipe to serendipity.

Companies like Google, Zappos, and even advertising agencies are trying to engineer serendipity. From the architecture of their buildings to where they put the beer machines to designated time for employees to focus on their passion projects, everything is designed to enable these seemingly chance innovations. Substantial research supports the concept that the best ideas bubble up when people have the opportunity to mingle and bring different ideas and skillsets to the table. This isn't just a zeitgeisty thing to do—it helps the bottom line.

All of this makes sense. Ideas build upon ideas. Anyone who has ever sat in a productive brainstorming session knows the concept well. There can be tons of bad ideas, but then something is triggered, sometimes from a random thought or idea that had been percolating in someone's mind for a while. It mixes with other ideas and BOOM—a truly fantastic concept can take shape.

PUSHING BOUNDARIES AND CREATING OPPORTUNITIES

Years ago, Google famously created a 20 percent time program for its engineers, called "Innovation Time Off." For every four hours that engineers spent working on a project for Google, they were required to spend one hour on their own passion project. Having the mental and physical space to let ideas brew is not only liberating, but it is also one of the fundamental pieces to creating the right atmosphere for innovation. This space to let creativity cook can also lead to the "adjacent possible," a concept coined by theoretical biologist Stuart Kauffman to explain biodiversity, among other things. It's a prescribed way in which biological progress happens. Kauffman describes this as the "untapped potential of what could be." In his book, Steven Johnson takes this idea further and applies it to society: "The adjacent possible is a kind of shadow future, hovering on the edges of the present state of things, a map of all the ways in which the present can reinvent itself," he writes.[2]

Johnson describes it as a house that magically expands with each door that you open—one room leading into more rooms. Those rooms are the adjacent possible. The idea is that the boundaries expand as you explore them. Successful engineers, scientists, entrepreneurs, academics, and artists all push boundaries, and it's these discoveries that lead to things like penicillin, Post-its, and Gmail.

So how can we make the "adjacent possible" in our careers? How do we push boundaries so that doors will open and lead us to unexpected opportunities? How can we orchestrate those unexpected-yet-positive outcomes and drive our own serendipity? "The trick is to figure out ways to explore the edges of possibility that surround you," writes Johnson. "This can be as simple as changing the physical environment you work in or cultivating a specific kind of social network, or maintaining certain habits in the way you seek and store information."[3]

THE SERENDIPITY FORMULA

Serendipity relies on a social network too. If ideas live in a vacuum, they will rarely come to fruition. A combination of forces take an idea and make it real. Social and professional networks can help drive ideas forward, and on an individual level they can give you the emotional or professional support you need. "There's the serendipity that takes place in your own head and then the serendipity from social," says Greg Lindsay, author of the upcoming book *Engineering Serendipity.* "It's really the mental state to put yourself into a situation where you might be surprised or you'll have an unexpected goal. But you also have to have the mental preparedness to recognize both the moment as significant enough, and then be able to actually exploit that moment. It's a process."

This is where someone like Michael Salort thrives. He understands the process and sees the opportunity. He actively puts himself into situations where an unexpected moment of good fortune can occur. He doesn't only go to events in the tech space, he also frequents entertainment functions. He attends screenings and book parties and makes sure to stay for the after-events. Whether it's another job opportunity or just a good connection for his professional network, Michael is mentally prepared for these moments because of his experience, diverse skillset, and ability to read the room.

Michael even has his own formula for serendipity: $\frac{(a + c - f) \times L}{v}$ = serendipity. In Michael's formula, a is "availability," c is "connections," f is "fear factor," L is "location," and v is "vision." He says that vision should be the number one because it needs to be singular and focused. If you have more than one vision, the focus gets diluted. "The key is to make yourself available and create connections, and then take out the fear factor," Michael says. "You multiply this times location. If you want to work in Hollywood, you can't live in Nebraska."

Remain Open and Ready

Michael agrees that your mental state is critical to creating professional serendipity. It starts with being open to new ideas and pushing your own boundaries so you can drive those opportunities and be able to seize the moment if something presents itself. And don't underestimate the ability to work the room. "You need to be skillful in social and professional settings and be incredibly charming," Michael says. "Even if it's not entirely natural, you have to push yourself to the highest possible charm level."

Finding ways to marry what you do with others' talents and push outside your own skillset is important. Michael can be at an entertainment event talking to someone about a script that he's developing, and then segue to the fundraising he's doing for a tech start-up that streams video. He plays matchmaker with people in the room and is always thinking about how what he does and who he knows could somehow benefit the person he's talking to. He broadens his personal narrative so he can find more connections with people he meets—connections that at first may not seem so obvious.

There's no doubt that this is an art. But it's something that you can learn to do, even if it doesn't come easily at first. It's not just working the room, but understanding how what you do fits in and how you can take what you know and apply it in different directions. "Be receptive to playing with other ideas, and look for how they branch with what your real core skillset or industry is," suggests Greg Lindsay. "Then once you find this weird hybrid, the final step is the ability to recognize how to use your personal network to amplify these ideas and figure out who can help you. The ability to discover people outside of your core network and develop them is really important."

Networking is a strategic skill. Not everyone likes to do it. In fact, many people hate it. Michael abides by the give-and-take principle of networking reciprocity: I scratch your back, you scratch mine. "You have to approach an event or a dinner party like a barter system, even though you're not saying it that way. It's like you're swapping eggs and milk," Michael says. "You need to show your eggs first and see who is willing to offer something, and present your value quickly without looking needy. You want to be perceived like you have a surplus of goods, and you want to get something out of it too."

Social Serendipity

For years, Michael would invite me to have drinks with him and other colleagues after work. I usually declined. I had young kids at home and didn't want to miss bedtime. After working all day, an after-work event seemed like more work and something I was not really up for. But Michael always saw these events as an extension of his day—perhaps the most important part of his day. It was at these cocktail parties and meetups that his network developed and flourished.

As Michael was networking, he was creating what Steven Johnson would call "a liquid network." Michael was maximizing the adjacent possible—opening doors for himself that would lead to all types of places. "Social serendipity requires getting out of your comfort spot and dabbling in other areas," Lindsay says. "Go to these strange events that are outside of your comfort zone, which also goes along with the notion of taking time for yourself. Invest the time and energy, and focus on who is going to be at these events."

Michael also gives himself the mental space to work on all kinds of projects—from purely creative to business-driven. He connects with his network to help drive those ideas through. He is always leveraging one project into something new. A script Michael wrote five years ago may be dormant until he meets a new producer and pitches the idea, and suddenly it has legs again.

Strategic Serendipity for Women

It turns out that Michael's good fortune was not wild luck at all, but actually a proven strategy that can be analyzed and measured—one that historically works. But do these principles translate to women? Or to moms with children at home? Or is our reality just different? Aside from opting to go to the cocktail party after work rather than getting home for bedtime, most moms I know aren't noodling with a host of creative projects. They just don't have the mental bandwidth—or the time or support—at least not when their kids are young.

"I think women in general are penalized in American society by not being able to take time for themselves to explore and think and play, particularly working mothers who are forced to maximize efficiency and who are focused on checking off every task," Lindsay says. "I think women need in general to carve out space for themselves to really be reflective and explore all of these things."

And that, of course, is the rub. We need the time to *take* time to engineer our serendipity. I don't love networking. I've never done enough of it—or enough of it all that well. When my kids were little and I was working at a PR agency, part of my job was to host and attend media events at night. I dreaded them, but made a conscious decision that if I had to miss bedtime and not see my kids, then I needed to double down and make sure I made the time worthwhile. At each event, I was determined to walk away with at a minimum two new media contacts. In the PR world, your relationships with editors, reporters, and TV producers are your career currency. If I had to miss out on my kids, I would maximize my career growth. I was strategic and intentional about it—spending time to figure out who was in the room and how I would connect with them.

I think most working moms try to become more efficient at work because we reprioritize what's important. It can be hard to figure out the value of an optional after-hours networking event. We no longer have the luxury of time to get a few cocktails, mingle, and hope to meet someone who can (maybe, one day) help us. It's too theoretical. A crapshoot. And if that event or conference costs money or requires travel, it may be even more difficult to justify. So we need to pick wisely, act strategically, and like Michael does, stay visible—even if it's not as often as we would hope.

PASSION AND PIVOTS PAVE THE WAY

Fifteen years ago when Michael was first getting into the tech space, Aminatou Sow was first learning to speak English. Born in Guinea to parents who were diplomats, Amina grew up in West

Africa and Europe and didn't speak English until she was a sophomore in high school. She went to the University of Texas at Austin in 2004 where she immersed herself in everything American, from pop culture to politics. When she graduated, she moved to Washington, DC, not having a job or even knowing anyone. Amina got an offer to be a press intern in then Senator John Kerry's office and was thrilled about the internship—only to be shocked to discover it was unpaid. After putting herself through college, there was no way she could work for free. "I had to go back to the drawing board about what I wanted to do," Amina says.

It was 2008 and the recession was in full force and taking a toll on recent graduates. Many of Amina's friends were unemployed. Amina took a job at a toy store in Georgetown.

"Nothing could crush your ego more than being in a status-driven town and not having a job in the industry that you want," Amina says. But she was optimistic and took advantage of the flexibility that came with working at the toy store. It gave her time to research different jobs, and she sent out her résumé all over DC.

At the end of that winter, Amina interviewed at the think tank New America, then called the New America Foundation. The only opening was an admin position, but Amina took the gig at the front desk and within a year moved over to its communications department. Amina, who cared about policy issues, soon realized she had a real knack for translating wonky policy into civilian engagement and making it a fun experience. "I was one of the few people who knew how to do website stuff. So I decided that was going to be my talent," Amina says.

Seeking New Challenges

The social media work she was doing took off, but Amina realized there wasn't really a place for her in the think tank world.

She knew she wanted to learn more about social media and social engagement, so she moved to a media strategy firm. From there, she was approached by the Iraq and Afghanistan Veterans of America (IAVA), a nonprofit organization that recruited her to lead its digital engagement. She didn't know anything about the U.S. military culture, but as a child of diplomats Amina felt an instant affinity toward military families. She also embraced the challenge. "When I was interviewing, I said, 'If you can get me to care, you can make anybody care.' I think that's how I got my job." Amina says.

Amina helped get legislation supporting veterans passed through Congress. "It's the job that I am most proud of," she says.

In the meantime, Amina, like Michael Salort and the Google engineers with their 20 percent Innovation Time Off, always had a passion project on the side. For Amina, it started with blogging in 2009 about the hunky White House Office of Management and Budget Director, Peter Orszag. Orszag defined the nerdy cool of the Obama administration, had a devoted following in DC—a following that read Amina's blog Orszagasm.com—and was profiled in *The New York Times*.

"One of my steadfast rules, no matter where you work: You need one project that's just for you and that's fun to do," Amina says. "I always had a knack for doing one fun thing on the side. It keeps you sane and keeps you happy and helps you flex your muscles and learn about other things."

"Don't Tell Me What Women Can't Do!"

In 2011, Amina was working at a digital firm with her friend Erie Mayer and launched Tech LadyMafia, a listserv to support and connect women in technology. This was a place to talk about salaries, jobs, or simply what they were doing in the tech world. Tired of hearing how unfriendly the tech space was to women and how few women worked in STEM, Amina wanted to do something about it.

"People kept telling us that there were no women in tech, and I thought that was crazy because I knew two women who were applying to be NASA astronauts," Amina said. "So we sent an email to twenty people and now it's grown to two thousand people around the world."

In 2014, Amina was at a party with her friend, the writer Ann Friedman, when a man told them that women don't podcast because they don't have enough patience to create them. "Nothing makes me do something faster than telling me that women don't know how to do something," Amina says. So this conversation, sparked by a pseudo dare, galvanized Amina and Ann to launch and cohost what became the wildly popular *Call Your Girlfriend*—a weekly podcast where smart women chew on interesting, timely topics ranging from politics to pop culture. With nearly 150 thousand downloads, the podcast has become a sensation, spreading largely through word of mouth and the tremendous press it has received. What started as a labor of love has become one of the go-to podcasts for women.

"We've been really surprised by the response. It confirms people want more female voices and people care about things that are presented in a casual and fun tone," Amina says.

Now thirty-two, Amina lives in San Francisco, and after leading political and social impact marketing for Google, has recently started her own consultancy. Google is now a client.

Perfect Timing for Serendipity

In Malcolm Gladwell's best-selling book *Outliers: The Story of Success*, he describes how timing impacts success. For Canadian hockey players, being born between January and March is the magic window if you're looking to turn pro because of the calendar cutoff for youth hockey league teams. The advantage goes to the older kids, who are usually the bigger kids, even in those early years of playing. And for tycoons of industry including the Rockefellers, Carnegies, and J.P. Morgan, Gladwell finds that simply being alive at the right time can greatly increase your odds of success. "Success is not a random act. It arises out of a predictable and powerful set of circumstances and opportunities..." writes Gladwell.[4]

In a very *Outliers* kind of way, Amina believes that she was born at just the right time—and she's probably right. Her timing for entering the world of social media was perfect. "If I were born even a year later, I don't think I would be where I am," Amina says. "I'm really cognizant of that. I think it was the right moment at the right time combined with not having too much fear."

But as we've seen from serendipity, Amina engineered her own "happy accidents" by maximizing good timing with the opportunities that came her way and nurturing relationships and networks. She sees the "adjacent possible" and pushes her own boundaries, which ultimately open up still more opportunities for her. "I'm such a proponent that you can do any job, aside from flying a rocket, with proper training and proper curiosity and just applying yourself. It always surprises me how many times people say, I could never do that. And I'm like, actually, you probably can."

Without realizing it, Amina is also applying Michael Salort's formula for serendipity. She makes herself open to new experiences and will take on projects outside of her skillset. She doesn't let fear prevent her from exploring something new. In fact, she loves the challenge. And Amina's approach to her career is exactly what experts say is the new way to think about our jobs.

"For me, it's more important to stay relevant than it is to worry about a career arc," Amina says. "I think about what are the skills that people will still need and what are the things that are useful?

Even in the work that I do at Google or the work I do in consulting on the side, I'm finding that people come to me about things that are completely outside of my skillset. People will say, 'You seem like a capable, connected person. What do you think about this?' Thinking about your career in terms of what problems do I want to solve and what do I want to be at the heart of?—and then seeing, well, here are the skills that I have and here is what I want to build on, and how can I contribute to all of those places?—is probably a better way to look at your career."

"When You Shine, I Shine"

People who know Amina agree that she defines badass. She moved to America on her own just three years after learning English. By the time she was twenty-eight years old, she was recognized as one of *Forbes*'s "30 Under 30" for technology. Her innovative work has supported US military veterans, and her eclectic group of interesting friends includes actress Lena Dunham. But what further defines Amina is that she loves encouraging women to take chances. One of her goals has been to create a stronger and more connected squad of women and to codify ways to help other women succeed. For Amina, it's natural. She's smart, social, and fierce. She is also incredibly generous.

The Tech LadyMafia's operating principle is Shine Theory: "When you shine, I shine." Forget about female competition where we loathe women who seem more together and accomplished than we are. This is about having the smartest and strongest women in your corner. Instead of feeling intimidated or threatened by an intelligent, witty, successful—and yes, even gorgeous—woman, befriend her. The idea is that when you look good, I look good.[5] This flips the catfight concept on its head. Women are not competing against each other for a limited slice of the pie. Instead, the ethos of Tech LadyMafia is to support the sisterhood and pay it forward. If you turn something down, you should pass it along to someone in your network. "It's an easy way to hook up other women with opportunities," Amina says.

Ask, Offer, and Receive

They also have a rule called "ask and offer," introduced by Tech LadyMafia member Natalia Oberti Noguera. Any time you go to a Tech LadyMafia event, you're supposed to ask for one thing, whatever you may need help with, and then you give something in return. Amina says that women often don't like to ask for help and appear needy. They can also be a little squeamish about offering something in return. "Even the act of saying it out loud to each other has been a huge game changer," Amina says.

Amina wants to reform the way women approach networking. Instead of seeing it as something obnoxious and aggressive, she wants women to have the space to brag about themselves, talk about their work, and yes, be self-promotional.

"When men get together, all they do is talk about work and that's how they know what's going on and what they need help with," Amina says. "When women get together, the talk is often about caretaking. When it comes to work, we never want to be seen as a burden or needing help, and I think professionally that attitude is a huge detriment. So I think that codifying asking and giving and talking about ourselves in a different way when we hang out with each other has been really important. And knowing that there is space to do that always helps to put people front of mind. When you feel that you are giving as much as you're taking, then what's the harm?"

In *The New York Times* best-seller *Give and Take: Why Helping Others Drives Our Success*, Adam Grant writes about giving as a new form of networking. This is not about the swapping eggs for milk reciprocity that Michael describes, but one in which the giver has a more long-term goal in mind. The approach: I'm here to help you because helping you may help me down the road. It may not, but it probably can.

"In traditional old-school reciprocity people operated like matchers, trading value back and forth with one another," Grant writes. "We helped the people who helped us, and we gave to the people from whom we wanted something in return. But today, there are givers who are sparking a more powerful form of reciprocity. Instead of trading value, these types of givers are looking to add value." And giving promotes giving. "Giving, especially when it's distinctive and consistent, establishes a pattern that shifts other people's reciprocity styles within a group."[6]

Amina is the quintessential giver, and she has created a network that could be a way to add value for everyone, not just to claim it for herself. "That's why I think the network is so important. Because if you're doing it all by yourself, you're doing it in a void—but if you have the power of a list or the power of other women driving you, there's so much more that you can achieve," she says.

Networks like Amina's have tremendous long-term impact. They are redefining the rules of engagement for women. They are showing women how to brag and ask for help and share their resources. They are encouraging women to share opportunities and pass along projects they may be passing on. We shouldn't hoard, we should give—because when you shine, I shine.

HACKING NETWORKING EVENTS AND GETTING VISIBLE

Amina's model is a more female-friendly one than the traditional post-conference cocktail party events that Michael navigates so well. But nonetheless, those industry events are where serendipity can be created and new opportunities discovered. The rub is that women often don't have the time to go to these events. We may even underestimate their importance. The key then is to be selective and strategic and sometimes even force ourselves to get out there, because visibility is the first step.

Conferences, many of us know, can be a time suck and a waste of money. Greg Lindsay recommends trying to get a visible role at a conference. Snag a speaking part if possible, or volunteer to help organize the conference and be involved in it. This is the perfect way to get connected and be introduced to some of the key players attending. Being a participant, rather than just an attendee, immediately elevates your profile and opens doors. The after-conference networking parties are also vastly more important than sitting in the sessions. Again, finding a conference organizer who can make some introductions for you is the perfect way to maximize these events without having to spend a day or more silently listening to speaker after speaker.

There are other places to create these connections too. Now, more than ever, there are opportunities to get out and mingle in settings that inspire fortuitous interactions that can lead to our own breakthroughs: new business ideas, projects, or other creative endeavors. Lindsay suggests joining a shared workspace like WeWork and really leaning on the community managers to introduce you to new people. These environments are designed for collaboration and cross-pollination of skillsets. You can discover the adjacent skills you want to learn and open your eyes to other possibilities. "As far as social serendipity is concerned, there's a whole new thing that's available to women now, which is real shared work environments with peer groups and meetups and all sorts of interesting networks," Lindsay says.

Knowledge is power, and knowing that you can manage your own good fortune—at least to an extent—is empowering. By putting yourself in the right places and putting energy into making strategic contacts and opening yourself up to what's out there, you can become the queen of your own serendipity.

4

NETWORKING IN THE GIRLS' LOUNGE
The Power of Connections

"If you want to go fast, go alone. If you want to go far, go with others."

—AFRICAN PROVERB

IN A HILTON HOTEL SUITE high over Midtown Manhattan, Shelley Zalis, fifty-three, is rearranging the furniture. It's tighter quarters than she is used to for her Girls' Lounge, and a crowd of women from the Advertising Research Foundation (ARF) conference downstairs is expected to come up for a lunchtime conversation. Undeterred by her high black wedge booties, Shelley is maneuvering some large sofas and hoisting coffee tables to make space for the dozens of women who will be attending her professional-empowerment-meets-girlfriend hangout. The Girls' Lounge soft-launched in a Las Vegas hotel room in 2012 and is Shelley's answer to the proverbial boys' club. It's a place where all businesswomen, at no charge, can mingle, network, and be pampered between conference seminars.

In an adjoining room, a pop-up Bliss spa lounge offers women free oxygen facials. The bathroom is stocked with hairstylists sprucing up blowouts. There's a manicurist doing polish changes and a makeup artist for a post-facial makeover. A cheerful woman is promoting her probiotic food line. And a company that rents high-end gowns, handbags, and jewelry is showcasing its couture and bling. There is even a perky "confidence coach" meandering around to help women boost their mojo, just in case it needs boosting.

How I got invited to the Girls' Lounge may best explain the essence of what this space is all about. In fact, in many ways it was the ultimate serendipity. It started in a buffet line at a bat mitzvah in Englewood, New Jersey, when a woman with a dazzling toothy smile introduced herself. Gilly Garrett and I had heard of one another over the years through our mutual friend, Sharon, the bat mitzvah girl's mom.

Gilly knew that I was a writer and asked what I was working on. I mentioned this book, and immediately Gilly exclaimed that I had to come with her to the Girls' Lounge event that Tuesday in New York. Gilly didn't work in advertising research. In fact, she didn't even know for sure what the conference was about. But Gilly told me enthusiastically that Shelley Zalis was her mentor—a fairy godmother of sorts, advising her and helping her grow her business as she took her organic skincare line into Whole Foods. She and Shelley had recently met through a friend. And that's how things evolved—girlfriends of girlfriends connecting to pull each other up, with Shelley helping to spread the pixie dust.

Coincidentally, I had just read about the Girls' Lounge in *The New York Times*.[1] In fact, I was toting the story around in my laptop bag as a reminder to add Shelley to the list of women I hoped to interview. A few days later, I found myself walking into the Hilton hotel suite, where Shelley enveloped me in a giant mama-bear hug. When Gilly explained to Shelley how we met at a bat mitzvah and how I just happened to be carrying around the *Times* article because I wanted to interview her for this book, Shelley smiled and said knowingly, "Yes, this is just how things work. It was meant to be and we were meant to meet."

Shelley, who lives in Los Angeles, has that karmic energy and gravitational pull. You can sense that her orbit of women truly adore and respect her. Shelley is chief Lady Boss, guru, and mom of three grown children, a dimension of her identity she never hid in the corporate world, but instead embraced, even as CEO—*especially* as CEO. Shelley believes passionately that women naturally make the best leaders, because our inherent nature (the caring and sharing tendencies, the ones ironically dismissed as negative leadership traits) helps inspire others and fosters a positive work environment. Nurturing, collaborating, and team building can drive business and build relationships. And, as Shelley likes to say, companies do business with people—and relationships are everything.

Rising in the ranks in the mostly male world of research, Shelley was very conscious of the kind of company culture she wanted to build. She was a qualitative researcher who spent many years at Nielsen before founding the research company Online Testing Exchange (OTX) in 2000 to assess consumer interest in movie trailers and TV ads. Before it became trendy, Shelley was disrupting the paradigm of the office culture and creating a workplace that leaned into lifestyle as an operating principle. She blew up the idea of traditional corporate policies that didn't jibe with her life as a working mom. She says that instead of conforming to the rules, she was always changing them because they just didn't make sense to her. At OTX there were no time sheets because "they're stupid and people make that stuff up anyhow," Shelley says. Face time wasn't important; instead, the ethos was to get your work done and leave when you were done, but not to leave your team behind.

KNOW YOUR PRIORITIES AND AVOID REGRETS

"One of the company's rules was 'live with no regrets,' which translated into thinking forward and asking yourself, 'Will I feel bad that I missed my child's soccer game or my parents' anniversary?' And if the answer is yes, don't miss it," Shelley says. "I don't think there is any such thing as work-life balance. You have one life with many dimensions. It's not a fifty-fifty proposition. You have family and work and friends, and all of those things are important. When you go through different life stages, you need to prioritize those dimensions differently. I don't think there's any set rule. I think it's what life cycle you are at and how you mix and match those dimensions to make it work."

Shelley was the kind of boss who called each of her 250 employees every winter break to say thank you. Over the years, she says, she spoke to her employees' spouses, parents, and children. Her employees even started to expect the phone call and would sometimes beat Shelley, calling her first. That was the kind of boss Shelley was, and that was the kind of family atmosphere she fostered. It was intentional and authentic to Shelley. It also helped grow her business: The company transformed the industry, and in 2010 Shelley sold OTX to a French company for $80 million.

Part of the Girls' Lounge's ethos is for women to bring their "female" to the table and not apologize for it. Shelley insists that women in the boardroom provide a healthy counterbalance to the men, and it's not just the culturally correct thing that needs to happen—it's good for business. At OTX, Shelley created a culture where women could thrive.

Shelley also realizes that the tension of work life shows no signs of easing. "There is such a scarcity of jobs at the top that women have been conditioned unfortunately to act like men, to try to conform to the rules that they know don't work for their lifestyle," Shelley says. "Women get to the middle level of their career and at the same time have more responsibility at home; they have children or aging parents, and that's when the work-life balance issue comes in. So we are losing our best leaders to caregiving, and yet our best leaders are caregivers. We need to create a culture where the best leaders can rise to the top and not just opt out because the culture of the workplace doesn't work for them."

THE MOTHER AND DAUGHTER CONNECTION

One of the themes of the Girls' Lounge event I attended was the power of the mother/daughter relationship. Shelley is creating a storytelling moment where moms and daughters share what they mean to each other. Lisa Sun, a former McKinsey & Company consultant who went to Yale University at fifteen years old and launched her own empowerment-meets-online-female fashion business, Project Gravitas, talks about her mother as the ultimate Tiger Mom and her biggest fan. "Always bet on yourself," Lisa tells us her mom would say when Lisa was weighing the option of creating her own business. Lisa describes how before Project Gravitas went live, her mom, in Taiwanese tradition, paid a Buddhist monk fifty dollars to pray for the company and release an auspicious lantern into the sky. We FaceTime with Lisa's mom in Taiwan, who shares how proud she is of Lisa and all she has accomplished.

Next, it's another mother/daughter story that is all feel good and girl power, and everyone is tearing up, including Shelley. This may be the Girls' Lounge differentiator. It's not just a professional workshop for women. Here, the lines between the professional and the personal are blurred. As women, moms, and professionals, we are human Venn diagrams with overlapping circles. Our womanhood and motherhood influence every aspect of our lives. In this room, no one apologizes for how they feel. You have permission to be all of it, all at once.

THE POWER OF THE PACK

The Girls' Lounge began as a meeting spot at the 2012 International Consumer Electronics Show (CES) in Las Vegas. Shelley invited some women and told them to invite their girlfriends to meet in her hotel room. The idea came about because of the feelings of loneliness and invisibility that women can have at these massive conferences. She had felt it too, years earlier at Cannes Lions in France when she was a researcher trying to understand the media world. She went to Cannes Lions and saw that most people hang with groups they are comfortable with—and being alone can be miserable.

"I was walking the street and thinking that it's so difficult to want to be here because I'm not invited to anything. No one knows me in this sea of fifty thousand people," Shelley says.

So in Las Vegas at CES, Shelley reserved a king-size hotel room, and within twenty-four hours there were fifty women gathered in her room, jammed into the small space, showing each other their technology and gadgets. On day two, one hundred women showed up, and she moved to the penthouse suite of the Four Seasons. On day three, the group grew to one hundred fifty. "We were connecting the way women like to connect. We were having our hair and makeup done, but doing deals as well. It was an environment that felt right and happy and comfortable and fabulous," Shelley says. "Two remarkable things also happened. One, for the men who thought there were no women in technology—we changed that perception. When you're alone, you're invisible, but now we had the power of the pack. You show up at the Girls' Lounge and you leave with twenty new girlfriends, and you go back into that big conference and you're walking the floor together. We instantly raised our collective clout and confidence; the men noticed, and we felt powerful."

At CES, the power of the pack moment gelled for Shelley. She realized that the more women, the greater the energy and the more powerful the feeling. Knowing that you have a group of women with you, in a literal sense, at these conferences feels good. You're not alone. Shelley says that the original intention for the Girls' Lounge was to create a destination for women to connect and collaborate and to ultimately activate change together, altering the ecosystem. But what started as a moment at CES has turned into a movement. On March 8, 2016, First Lady Michelle Obama invited the Girls' Lounge to Washington, DC, to celebrate the Obama Administration's "Let Girls Learn" initiative, which helps adolescent girls worldwide attend and complete school. With only a few days' notice, Shelley had a bus transformed to serve as a mobile Girls' Lounge, this time for teenage girls. US Ambassador to the United Nations Samantha Power joined the traveling crew at an event celebrating girls' global education.

Now Shelley is taking the Girls' Lounge to corporations to create communities within companies so women can have a network of like-minded women with like-minded issues. "Women all have the same challenges," Shelley says. "It really is a gender conversation, mainly because we go through different life stages that are very different from men and we have a lot in common that we can share. I don't want women to feel like they should go back to being competitive to get ahead. The story should be about the impact of the collective and the power of collaboration and the impact of sharing what the collective brings to the table."

THE MODERN MULTI-HYPHENATE

"Happy International Women's Day!" Rachel Sklar cheerfully says when I meet her at a café in New York City's East Village, down the street from where her infant daughter is in daycare. It feels particularly apropos to be talking to Rachel, a woman who is strongly identified with elevating important social issues from feminism to diversity, on March 8, a day designated for recognizing influential women who effect change.

A proud Canadian born and raised in Toronto, Rachel moved to New York City in 1998 to practice corporate law at a white-shoe firm. Law school was never her dream, but rather a prudent plan influenced by Rachel's parents. Sometimes a burning passion mixed with a nagging feeling you may be in the wrong place has a way of bubbling up and stirring action in certain people, and Rachel is one of those people.

While practicing law, Rachel moonlighted in journalism— feeding her creative spirit that was largely dormant in her day-to-day proofing of legal documents. When one of her stories was published, she would dance around her law office, exhilarated to see her byline. Then in a punk-rock move, Rachel did what friends would call insane or brave—or both, depending on whom you asked. She quit her lucrative job (a job with a lovely secretary, a fat paycheck, and an almost certain career trajectory) to become a full-time freelance writer. Scrappy and driven, Rachel honed her writing skills, taking classes and freelancing for outlets including *Glamour* and *The New York Times* before landing a job in 2005 as Mediabistro's FishbowlNY blogger and editor. This put her smack dab inside the burgeoning world of New York's new media. Rachel's witty and incisive writing and reporting, together with her almost savant-like ability to network with just the right people at just the right time, had her rise through the online ranks from a blogger to a founding editor of *The Huffington Post*.

Rachel is a modern-day multi-hyphenate. She describes herself as a writer, entrepreneur, connector, and single mom—and if there is more space in the bio, she may throw in joke writer and showtune singer. A passionate musical theater fan, she's written and directed her own plays. She's also a sleepaway camp enthusiast. In many ways, sleepaway camp provided the foundation for Rachel's life; it was the summer birthplace of her creative expression and her "connector" savvy. Rachel's dogged enthusiasm for connecting, supporting, and lifting people dates back to Camp Winnebagoe in Ontario. "I was the queen of summer camp," Rachel says, smiling.

I first met Rachel in 2009 when I was working at a PR agency and my client was her new employer, the media start-up Mediaite. As its first employee and the founding editor, she helped to launch the site, founded from scratch by lawyer turned TV legal analyst Dan Abrams. Rachel's smart commentary and reporting on media, culture, technology, and social issues catapulted her to rock-star status in many circles—circles that I followed. She was also a regular on the cable shows, weighing in on a host of subjects. Articulate and spirited, with expressive green eyes, wavy chestnut hair, and a massive smile, Rachel was cable-TV perfect.

Long a champion of social issues, single motherhood is now another fabric woven into the quilt of Rachel's professional identity. While in her second trimester, Rachel wrote a much-talked-about piece for the publishing platform Medium about being single and pregnant at forty-one. "I had a lovely summer romance and got pregnant," she writes. "The relationship ended, the pregnancy did not."[2] Witty, poignant, and ballsy, Rachel ripped off the veil of secrecy and shame surrounding fertility, single motherhood, and a woman's age. Writing about her experiences, Rachel exposed the struggles, myths, and medical realities that women face. Even while pregnant (or perhaps, especially while pregnant), Rachel was helping to change the paradigm about what's expected and accepted for women.

Changing the Ratio: The Birth of a Network

In spring of 2010, Rachel cofounded Change the Ratio with Emily Gannett, with the goal to increase the visibility and opportunity for women in technology and new media. Rachel was a journalist with coding skills limited to HTML, but she had become a fixture in New York City's emerging digital scene in 2005. Change the Ratio was Rachel's response to women's lack of recognition in the world of start-ups and technology. A 2010 *New York* magazine article about the tech industry that profiled almost all white men was the trigger. Rachel emailed numerous women in the tech space, saying she was tired of writing the post-mortem "Where are the women?" stories. That email launched Change the Ratio, and its hashtag #changetheratio spawned momentum on Twitter and became the rallying cry for diversity in technology and other industries.

Its motto "Visibility begets access begets opportunity" inspired Rachel's next step, which she says was the natural evolution of visibility intersecting with opportunity. In 2012, Rachel and her friend and former writing colleague Glynnis MacNicol created TheLi.st, a membership network, listserv, and media platform. "It started to become very clear that it was not only useful for the women on it, but it was starting to be essential," Rachel says. "It was fulfilling a wide range of purposes. It became a quick pipeline for high-level crowdsourcing. When you are dealing with a highly vetted community, what you get is going to be of excellent quality. It was saving people time. If it came through TheLi.st, odds were it was well vetted."

In only a short time, TheLi.st had evolved into not just a list-serv, but a true community of women supporting women. Women posted heartfelt personal issues along with professional quandaries or discreet queries like, "What should my salary requirements be?" In true female form, TheLi.st became an online village for women to lift and encourage its members. And like Amina Sow's Tech LadyMafia network discussed in chapter 3, it became a space to brag, share, and let people know about women's accomplishments and what they were working on. "It's a network that's meant to literally amplify and propagate," Rachel says. "It's a place for message magnification."

Today, TheLi.st has about five hundred members. That is the sweet spot, Rachel believes, for keeping the community intimate enough to be helpful and serve the needs of its members. Unlike other women's networks that may be particular to a certain industry, TheLi.st is a group of generalists because, well, Rachel is a generalist, and she intersects with multiple circles. Many of the women are entrepreneurs, while others work in media, culture, academia, and technology.

In the spirit of full disclosure, I should admit that I am a member. I have experienced first-hand the power of an engaged platform of supportive women. The women on TheLi.st have provided encouragement, insight, and interviews for this book. They have exposed me to people and ideas I wouldn't have come across on my own. They have offered advice and even helped with a title when I was told that my original working title was already taken.

Female networks aren't new—in fact, they are intrinsic to who we are as women. From helping women give birth to nursing each other's babies to supporting our sisters in the proverbial village, women have always helped women. But the idea of a professional network is relatively new and, as Rachel says, it's important for society as a whole.

"Men have always had strong professional networks and women have always had strong personal networks, but because historically there were fewer women in the workforce and because there are fewer women as you go up the ladder, there are fewer people to network with," Rachel says. "It becomes more important to really make sure you are nurturing the next generation of talent and that you're watching out for fairness; not just because it's a social good, but because it makes the system better, which makes the output better, which is better for society."

THE ROLE OF SUPERCONNECTORS

Rachel's had an oversized impact on many people's careers and professional relationships. She's a name that comes up when people are thinking of writers and speakers who straddle feminist issues, media, technology, and culture. Because she's well known and influential in multiple arenas, it's perhaps no surprise that Rachel is the ultimate connector. As Malcolm Gladwell points out in *The Tipping Point: How Little Things Can Make a Big Difference,* a connector holds a crucial position in society. A connector can be the reason that trends take off, businesses thrive, restaurants do well, and people get jobs. A connector simultaneously sits at the apex and intersection of just about everything.[3] In the book, Gladwell describes connectors who are influencers. These are the people whose many acquaintances span across social circles and who can help in the spreading of ideas. They are the people who also know everyone. "The point about connectors is that by having a foot in so many different worlds, they have the effect of bringing them all together," writes Gladwell.[4] "It isn't just the case that the closer someone is to a connector, the more powerful or wealthier or the more opportunities he or she gets. It's also the case that the closer an idea or a product comes to a connector, the more power and opportunity it has as well."

Shane Snow takes this idea further in his book *Smartcuts: How Hackers, Innovators, and Icons Accelerate Success*, where he names a subset of Gladwell's connectors as "superconnectors." Superconnectors actively use their networks to help individuals reach many people at once.[5] Rachel, who occupies multiple spaces and attracts interesting people, has a halo effect and a generosity that make her a superconnector.

There is another characteristic of influential people like Rachel who act not only as a bridge between people, but who also give in other types of professionally important ways. In his book *Give and Take*, Adam Grant writes that in traditional reciprocity, we helped the people who helped us. We gave expecting something of value in return. These people are what Grant calls "matchers." But, as we discussed in chapter 3, Grant writes about a more powerful form of giving that can prove more successful for people over the long haul.

"What I found most magnetic about successful givers: they get to the top without cutting down others, finding ways of expanding the pie that benefit themselves and the people around them. Whereas success is zero sum in a group of takers, in groups of givers, it may be true that the whole is greater than the sum of the parts," writes Grant.[6]

Rachel sees pieces of herself in what Grant describes. Giving has always come naturally to Rachel. "I think I'm somewhere between a giver and a matcher," she says, but adds that there is a limit to giving and warns about giving too much. Women, she says, are particularly at risk—because we don't like to say no.

"Giving all day every day all the time without any curbing of it is draining—and you need to move forward too," Rachel says. "And more to the point, it's always women who are expected to do this giving for free all of the time."

NETWORKING: THE POWER OF WE

In LinkedIn founder Reid Hoffman's *The Start-Up of You,* he describes how an individual's career accelerates with the help of his or her network. He gives it a formula too: "I" to the power of "We."[7] This in many ways is Rachel Sklar's and Shelley Zallis's model. Through Rachel's TheLi.st, the collective power of women can amplify messages. The women help each other grow professionally and support each other emotionally. They share advice, contacts, and job leads. They embody and embrace Rachel's motto, "Visibility begets access begets opportunity."

For Shelley, it's the power of the pack. When we physically show up together in a space, our confidence and clout grows. We are not invisible. As Amina Sow showed us with her Tech Lady-Mafia network in chapter 3, when we pay it forward and share our resources, we all win. Amina's mantra "When you shine, I shine" also acknowledges the power of We. Interestingly, the collective power isn't about close ties. In fact, studies show that it's not your closest friends or contacts that can accelerate your career; it's usually the "weak ties" that are the most important when it comes to finding job opportunities.

Why Weak Ties May Be the Best Ties

In sociology, the strength of weak ties is an established principle, going back to 1973 and research by Mark Granovetter at Johns Hopkins University. He found that the best job leads came from distant acquaintances, not close friends or family. That's because the closely knit groups you belong to are filled with people who know roughly the same things that you do.[8] You need to get outside of that space. You have to push outside of your core group. The weak tie is essentially the bridge to getting information.

In many ways, this is great news. Strong ties take a lot of energy to maintain. Those relationships need nurture and time to cultivate, time that most women—working moms in particular—don't have. Weak ties don't require nearly as much effort to keep up, and we can leverage them easily through social media or email. The networks that Rachel, Shelley, and Amina have created are essentially organized structures of weak ties. They pull from women in different industries, across the country—and even the world. Ironically, the network's influence is magnified because the ties are weak. And these networks are what can make women professionally more viable and accelerate their careers.

Finding and Building a Strong Network

Do a Google search on women and professional networks and you will get millions of hits. These days, there are all types of networking groups—from regional to national, online and off—for female entrepreneurs and specific industry professionals. Although many networks may be well intentioned, they don't all work equally. In fact, research from Stanford University and IDEO identified the ideal makeup of a network: "part pack rat, part librarian, and part good Samaritan."

"The pack rat brought a range of resources that could be accessed and used to create new and fresh ideas. The librarian brought information and knowledge. And the good Samaritan had the attitude and practice of sharing," writes Athena Vongalis-Macrow in her *Harvard Business Review* blog post "Assess the Value of Your Networks."[9]

The research found the key to a healthy network is the quality of the members and how often they communicate. Network strength can be measured by the relationships between the members and what each person brings to the table. Are they actively trying to help and share resources? Are they readily available and do they respond regularly? The frequency of communication is critical to an effective network.[10]

Within these groups are always those superconnectors like Rachel who can make introductions and build connections. I would argue that these days, having a mentor might be less important than having a superconnector in your life. Identifying your superconnector may not be obvious at first. But if you pay attention to who roams around the room, hopscotching around an event, and seems to delight in bringing people together, you can guess that she is a superconnector and someone you should meet. If the network interaction largely takes place online through message boards or listservs, see who is most active and willing to offer help. Reach out to that woman and, if possible, meet in person. She does not need to become your best friend— in fact, it's better if she doesn't. The power of weak ties tells us that we don't need to be super-close to our superconnectors for them to be meaningful.

There is an expression that the "fortune is in the follow up." Taking the time to follow up with people after you meet and seeing how you may help them too can be critical to cultivating a relationship. Pay attention to the conversation you have and see how you can help them network or solve a problem. Also remember to say thank you. It seems obvious, but many people forget to show gratitude. Even though that email you're asking your contact to write on your behalf may only take five minutes for her to write, it's taken ten years for her to build that relationship. Respect that.

When We All Win

Being connected to a group also impacts the willingness of people to actively help, especially when the giving is codified and almost expected. When these networks make it okay to ask and receive, everyone wins, says Adam Grant. The networks also reduce the drain Rachel said many women feel when they're always giving it away, feeling like they are expected to never say no.

"If a group develops a norm of giving, members will uphold the norm and give, even if they're more inclined to be takers or matchers elsewhere. This reduces the risks of giving: when everyone contributes the pie is larger, and givers are no longer stuck contributing far more than they get," writes Grant.[11]

Networks are not new, but their importance, particularly now as our economy becomes increasingly entrepreneurial, continues to grow. Rules of engagement that create a protocol of giving and matching are the proven methods for a "we-all-win" network. Playing the long game and knowing you may have to *give* before you *get* anything back is the best mindset to create a sustainable ecosystem that can ultimately help everyone.

LinkedIn is one of Silicon Valley's billion-dollar success stories. It took networking online and transformed how people found jobs and how they connected with each other. The new female networks have taken different approaches and arguably have a different ultimate end game. LinkedIn's mission statement says simply, "To connect the world's professionals to make them successful and productive." I would argue that a female network's goal must be more collective and kibbutz-like to be successful. We all contribute and we all benefit from each other's contributions. We take and give back. We have strength in numbers.

This isn't about altruism. As Grant writes, it's a cocktail of emotions that inspires people to give. At some point, everyone wants something in return. But as Shelley and Rachel have shown, we have more clout, confidence, and opportunity when we help each other. For women, it's not only about connecting; it's about pulling each other up as we rise together.

5

FALLING FROM THE TOP
Rising with Resilience

"A woman is like a tea bag—you never know how strong she is until she gets in hot water."

—ELEANOR ROOSEVELT

T'S MAY 14, 2015, EXACTLY a year to the day since sixty-one-year-old Jill Abramson, *The New York Times*'s first and only female executive editor, was very publicly fired from the top editorial post at the most prestigious newspaper in the nation. Two and a half years into her job, she was kicked to the curb so unceremoniously that her ouster made headlines around the world. It was the first time in the paper's 160-year history that a woman sat at the top of the masthead. So when Jill was fired, allegedly for her "brusque management style," the media went wild. Some reported that Jill was "difficult," which for a female executive is a word loaded with gender double standards. It was also reported that Jill had hired a lawyer before she was fired to look into compensation issues, believing that she was not paid the equivalent to her male predecessor.[1]

Coincidentally, on the first anniversary of Jill's dethroning, I heard her speak at the Women's Power Habits conference in New York City, run by Rachel Sklar and Glynnis MacNichol's

TheLi.st. (As mentioned in chapter 4, TheLi.st is a network and media platform devoted to empowering women.) Jill's one-on-one conversation with Rachel Sklar was fittingly named "Be the Disrupter, Not the Dinosaur."

Jill's session followed "Starting from the Bottom," an inspiring talk with Kathryn Minshew, the devastatingly smart twenty-nine-year-old CEO and cofounder of The Muse. Kathryn announced that she just closed a funding deal of $10 million for her job search-meets-career-advice start-up. Together with her cofounder, Alex Cavoulacos, Kathryn had taken The Muse from a scrappy jobs website for Millennials to a serious employment platform and online career resource that they are expanding into every major metro area in the country. The women in the audience exploded in applause.

"After listening to Kathryn and her impressive business, I thought maybe our talk should be called 'Falling from the Top,'" Jill says with a laugh. "One of the basic truths for just about everybody in the working world is that usually you will hit a roadblock and get fired from a job, and there's no reason not to call it what it is."

As a prominent journalist, Jill felt strongly that she wasn't going to sugarcoat her firing. She would own it. "I devoted my life to telling the truth through reporting, I was not going to try to put lipstick on it," Jill says.

NO SURRENDER: GET UP AND GO AFTER IT

Even with the tabloid media hounding Jill after she was fired, she didn't let herself feel shamed or collapse into a puddle about what was next. "I wasn't really prepared for the amount of attention that this got. *The New York Post* followed me when I was walking my dog," Jill says. "I tried to be good-natured and polite to all of these people. It mattered to me to try to set an example. Paralyzed with fear was not an option because this was public. I had accepted an invitation to be a commencement speaker at Wake Forest University. The person who arranged it had called me and said, 'I'm sure you will withdraw.' And I said, 'There's no way I'm going to withdraw. It was very important to me to show resilience to somehow convey my excitement about the future and the fact that I wasn't completely knocked off course.'"

The morning after Jill was fired, she went to a session with her trainer who handed her a pair of boxing gloves. She had never boxed before, but hitting the bag was intensely satisfying. Jill asked her trainer to take a picture of her with the gloves and she emailed it to her kids who were worried about her. "I wanted to show them that mom is in fighting form," Jill says.

Her daughter, Cornelia, posted the photo on Instagram and it went viral. The next day it was the cover of *The New York Post*. While she never intended anyone to see the photo except for her kids, Jill's message "get up and go after it" was something she was proud for the world to see. She wasn't defeated. She wouldn't disappear. Still fiercely passionate about her work, Jill would move forward. That meant returning to her love of writing, reporting, and teaching. Jill is now a political correspondent for *The Guardian*, and she's writing a book about how digital is transforming the newsroom. She is also teaching journalism classes at her alma mater, Harvard University.

"Cold calling people and trying to convince them to let me in and trust me as a reporter was scary because I hadn't done it in a while," Jill says. "I thought my way of doing it had probably somehow gone out of style as the journalistic firmament and the whole world of news is changing so dynamically and rapidly."

Speaking to a roomful of women, Jill admitted that going solo can be tough and scary and was not something that she was used to. "Sometimes it's lonely being out on your own," Jill says. "Sometimes I can feel like I am falling off the planet and maybe no one notices. I've been in newsrooms my whole life surrounded by other journalists. I miss that."

Writing a New Chapter: Harvard Yard and Daycare Drop-offs

Nearly a year after hearing Jill at the conference, we meet in her office in the basement of the Barker Center at Harvard. This is Jill's second year of teaching an intro to journalism seminar. The first thing that strikes you about Jill is her distinctive voice. It's an unusual voice that's been judged and dissected, even analyzed by scientists as to its origins. *The New Yorker's* Ken Auletta described it as a nasal car honk, an odd combination of upper and working class. When we meet, Jill is dressed in a simple black dress and cardigan sweater and is excited to be going to a party later that evening honoring novelist Toni Morrison, who has been guest lecturing at Harvard.

The night before, Jill was up half a dozen times with her six-month-old granddaughter, Eloise. During the week, Jill now lives with her daughter, Cornelia, thirty-three, and son-in-law Robert, thirty-two, in Boston. They are both surgical residents at Massachusetts General Hospital, with grueling work schedules. On the weekends, Jill goes home to Madison, Connecticut, where her husband Henry has recently been appointed the town historian. They also have a loft apartment in New York's Tribeca, but these days it's rarely used.

After getting fired, Jill made a conscious decision that while she would continue working, she wanted to control her own schedule and spend more time with her family, which now means helping care for Eloise. Aside from night duty, Jill will eventually do the drop-offs and pick-ups from daycare. "I want to do what I can to enable my daughter, who has such extreme work-life balance, to be the surgeon she wants to be," Jill says.

Getting Heard

The first year after losing her job was a year of reflection. Jill felt depressed. She ruminated. She dug deep. And she did what she warns other women never to do: "I rewound the movie and tried to examine where did I go wrong, what didn't I see in real time?"

But some of this replaying of the film in her mind, Jill says, was valuable. It unearthed the roots of her communication style, a style that she feels can be profoundly misunderstood. "I realized that for a lot of my career I felt unheard, which I think is a familiar thing to women," Jill says. "Often, I would make a point in a meeting, it would be ignored, and the boss would say, 'as Jerry said.' I think I talked too much and didn't listen enough, and that directness was interpreted as being intimidating. So I've tried to be more careful about both of those things."

What Jill describes, the feeling of being blown off in a meeting of mostly men or, worse, having your brilliant idea attributed to the guy at the table rather than you isn't only a remnant of old-school newsrooms. It's still a common phenomenon in classrooms, conference rooms, and even the White House. When President Obama took office in 2008, nearly two-thirds of his senior staff were men. The female staffers had a tough time not only being invited to important meetings, but also being acknowledged once they were there. So the women developed a genius strategy that they called "amplification." When one of the women at the meeting made a point, other women would repeat it and give credit back to the original contributor. "We just started doing it and made a purpose of doing it. It was an everyday thing," said one former Obama aide who requested anonymity to speak frankly to *The Washington Post*, which first reported on this story. It worked and President Obama started noticing and calling on more women in meetings.[2]

Survivor

Resilience and grit are inherent to Jill. In a quite literal sense, she is a survivor. On May 7, 2007, as she was crossing the street on her way to the gym, Jill was run over by a delivery truck in New York. The truck crushed her right foot. The rear tire ran over her left side, breaking her femur and pelvis and leaving her with severe internal injuries. A titanium rod was inserted into her leg, and she endured months of painful rehabilitation and recovery, moving from a wheelchair to crutches to a cane before recovering. Years later, she even wrote a piece in *The New York Times* about the traumatic experience and its residual effects. The piece was published less than two weeks before she was fired.[3] Perhaps losing a job is all about perspective. After having been run over by a truck, you define your life differently.

Jill was devastated when she was fired, but she didn't panic. She took a walk through Central Park and had dinner with her family that night. She knew she didn't have to be "Jill Abramson from *The New York Times*" to survive. She was a survivor already.

During 2016, as a political columnist for *The Guardian*, Jill covered the presidential campaign, focusing on Hillary Clinton's second bid for the White House. Jill first met the Clintons in 1978 when she was working as a freelance writer at a political consulting firm in South Carolina and Bill Clinton was running for governor of Arkansas. She has reported on both Clintons for decades. It's not simply being of a similar age and professional status that makes Jill feel a kinship toward Hillary—it's also that unwinnable double bind where a woman's leadership style, vocal tone, and likability are scrutinized and questioned that connects them.

"Personal qualities are much more commented on when you are a woman in power than a man," Jill says. "I identify with that. It also has occurred to me that some of these things, which have not changed in my lifetime in the workplace, may change with a woman president."

Get on with Your Knitting

Jill scored a series of firsts in female leadership roles after joining *The New York Times* in 1997. She served as the first female Washington Bureau Chief, the first female Managing Editor, and the first female Executive Editor. Ironically, Jill discovered that it was losing her job at the top of the *Times*'s masthead that suddenly made her a visible role model for women, particularly younger women. The press frenzy that swirled around her firing, and climaxed at her memorable Wake Forest commencement address days after being fired, showcased Jill as a fierce woman who flexed her grit with grace and balanced it with humor. In her speech, Jill spoke about the importance of continuing to work— to always grow and create. She invoked the commencement speech Robert Frost gave to Colby College in 1956.

"He described life after graduating as a piece of knitting to go on with. What he meant is that life is always unfinished business, like the bits of knitting women used to carry around with them, to be picked up in different intervals," Jill told the 2014 Wake Forest graduates. "So today you gorgeous, brilliant people, get on with your knitting."[4]

Most people probably won't fall as far in their careers as Jill Abramson did when getting fired as executive editor of the *Times*, but her commencement message was clear: Never give up on yourself or your life's work.

"I really believe in that Robert Frost poem. You've got to pick yourself up, and if you have had a good career until that point, launch something off of that. Life would be boring if it was just one arc of success. People do show what they are made of when something bad happens to them, like getting fired," Jill says. "I think in some ways my having been fired has been a much more powerful message, especially to younger women, than being the executive editor of the *Times*. I get stopped on the street by younger women who say, 'Thank you for what you did, I admire you so much.' And I don't think they are talking about just having been the Executive Editor, and that's very meaningful to me," Jill says.

Personal Ink Tells a Story

When Jill got fired, much was made about what she would do with the "T" (for the *Times*) tattoo she recently had inked onto the middle of her back by a tattoo artist in the East Village. Jill assured everyone that the tattoo wasn't going anywhere. It's emblazoned into her skin as much as it's burned into her identity—and by the way, it's not the only tattoo Jill has. At fifty years old, when Jill was promoted from Washington Bureau Chief to Managing Editor, she moved back to New York City and marked the milestone by getting a tattoo of a New York subway token. She wanted something quintessentially New York, and because she loved the subway and didn't want an apple tat, she got the token. A decade later, on the cusp of turning sixty, Jill got the now famous "T" for the Times and "H" for Harvard stacked on top of each other on her back. She also got a tattoo of a South Carolina palmetto tree, an ode to her time post-college when she and her husband lived in South Carolina and worked for progressive political candidates.

"I think of them as my personal hieroglyphics, and they all relate to something in my life, like a passage," Jill says, taking off her sweater and showing me the art on her back. "It was just a passion that seized me out of nowhere. No one in my family particularly approved. My husband was like if you really want to get one, go ahead."

Most sixty-year-old women are probably not getting inked. But most are not Jill Abramson. She wants to be thought of as a helluva reporter who was gutsy and inspired her colleagues to dig deeper than deep and be fearless about informing the public. Being a woman at the top of the masthead remains meaningful to Jill, and pulling women up with her has always been important. She actively sought to bring gender balance and diversity to the newsroom. She increased the number of female editors on the masthead to 50 percent. She wants to be known as a woman who helped other women achieve what they dreamed of achieving in journalism. And she wants others to know that she knows she's not perfect.

"I'm not some kind of Joan of Arc, and I would like it to be known that I was open to the fact that I've made some mistakes too," Jill says.

Jill thoroughly loves her time teaching and hopes to inspire the next generation of curious, brave, and extraordinary journalists. And it's in this next chapter of her life that she feels like she's continuing to make a difference. Jill thinks of her dad when she talks about dealing with getting through the tough times. "He was always proud of my accomplishments, but he was more proud of how my sister and I handled setbacks," Jill says. "It's during those times he would say, 'That's how you show what you're made of.'"

It can be easy to say that Jill would land on firm ground. She's been on *Fortune's* Most Powerful Women list; she is one of the most seasoned and respected newspaper reporters and editors in America; she landed a million-dollar book deal, a teaching gig at Harvard, and a columnist position at *The Guardian*, where she's covering politics. But she's sixty-one years old in an era where forty-one can feel over the hill, particularly in the media industry.

"A career is a long arc, and it's so easy to lose track of that. You're under pounding pressure to carpe diem like several times in a week," Jill says. "Keep your patience, because looking back on things, opportunity doesn't knock just once. Sometimes you pass by a career opportunity because it isn't right because of your family life or other reasons. Another opportunity will come along. Opportunity and time go together and are your friends; keep that in mind."

6

CONGRATULATIONS, YOU'RE FIRED!

'VE BEEN FIRED—MORE THAN ONCE. The first time was during the first Clinton Administration, when I was a Capitol Hill press secretary working for US Congressman Peter DeFazio from Oregon. I had left another press secretary job with US Congressman Peter Deutsch from South Florida after a year and a half to join DeFazio's team. Making only $20,000 a year with Deutsch, the raise to $25,000 was incentive enough to switch Peters. I had college loans to pay, was completely on my own financially, and was living with my boyfriend who was paying our rent.

What I didn't realize when I took the gig was that DeFazio was more Libertarian than Democrat and he insisted that every press release read "DeFazio Bashes Clinton on _____ fill-in-the-blank." Having served as the college president of Students for Clinton a few years earlier at Northwestern University, this was a bad ideological fit for both of us. So at twenty-three years old, after six months on the job, I was fired. Embarrassed and shocked, I didn't look for another gig on the Hill but waited tables at an

Italian restaurant in Bethesda, Maryland. A few months later, I got married to the boyfriend, backpacked around Southeast Asia, and then moved to New York, where I landed my first job in television as an investigative assistant producer.

About fifteen years later, I got fired again: this time, from a tech start-up. Here, I was told it was a culture thing, which in tech parlance means that they just don't like you very much. They kept me on for another six months as a consultant because while they may not have liked my personality, they liked my writing.

Kick ahead another few years, and I get fired a third time—this time from a digital media start-up. Here, I was told everyone liked me, at least most people did, but I was just too darned expensive. At my exit meeting, my manager, who was in preschool when I was in high school, said they could hire three people for my salary. She pointed to a senior-level twenty-seven-year-old who was successfully running multiple pieces of their multi-million-dollar business and earning a little more than half of what I made. That twenty-seven-year-old was an exceptionally talented guy—but the fact that they couldn't find another place for me given how "smart, creative, and strategic" they believed I was reinforced the point. At a company of Millennials, I was too old and expensive for them to see a "fit" or try to find one. They also assured me that I wasn't really getting fired, we were just separating—as if it were mutual and maybe one day, when they were ready, we would get back together again.

THE DISPOSABLE EMPLOYEE

In an April 2016 article in *The New York Times*, "Congratulations! You're Fired," Dan Lyons discusses the bizarre and cruel culture of the start-up HubSpot, where he worked for almost two years. He describes how the tech world's ethos is infecting corporate cultures everywhere.[1]

"When you got fired, it was called 'graduation.' We all would get a cheery email from the boss saying, 'Team, just letting you know that X has graduated and we're all excited to see how she uses her superpowers in her next big adventure,'" Lyons writes.[2]

Lyons describes this surreal ritual at HubSpot, where he landed after getting laid off from *Newsweek* after twenty-five years in journalism. Lyons wasn't fired from HubSpot; he left voluntarily. In his book *Disruption: My Misadventure in the Start-Up Bubble* he writes about the cultish frat vibe of HubSpot and the way it treats its employees as disposable widgets who can be replaced and discarded. Sadly, this approach may not be unique to HubSpot. It is becoming accepted—not just at tech companies, but across corporate America. In a modern workplace of all-you-can-eat organic snacks and Belgian beer gardens, it turns out that old-fashioned job loyalty is as retro as the company's Xerox machine.

"They see Silicon Valley as a model of enlightenment and forward thinking, even though this 'new' way of working is actually the oldest game in the world: the exploitation of labor by capital," Dan Lyons writes in *The New York Times*. "Unfortunately, working at a start-up all too often involves getting bossed around by undertrained (or untrained) managers and fired on a whim. Bias based on age, race and gender is rampant, as is sexual harassment."[3]

TOUR OF DUTY

Because the tech culture is influencing the old guard in how they treat and relate to their employees, the social contract is getting even more flimsy. People can be fired, laid off, separated—you name the euphemism. The bottom line: There is zero job security anymore.

Workers in tech companies are "serving a tour of duty" that might last a year or two, writes LinkedIn founder Reid Hoffman in his book *The Alliance: Managing Talent in the Networked Age.* Companies dispose of people when someone better or cheaper comes along. The goal, Hoffman writes, is to strategically leverage your tour of duty so it aligns to the goals of the company and betters yourself as well.[4] Get what you need, do some good work, and prepare to move on. The honeymoon won't last. This is either depressing or empowering, depending on your age and probably your reliance on a steady income.

"We're a team, not a family" is the corporate mantra that emerged from Netflix in 2009.[5] This Netflix code has apparently been adopted by other companies, including HubSpot: They invest in you when it's working and dump you when it's not. Lyons also describes a data-driven metric called value over replacement player (VORP) that the company uses for evaluating employees. It's cold metrics for sizing up an employee's worth. It came from baseball, where owners set prices on different players. Clearly, this is no family. And sadly, this type of employer/employee relationship, Lyons writes, is becoming the new normal.

In chapter 4, Shelley Zalis talked about how she ran her company OTX like a family. Her business was rooted in a very female notion of caring and sharing. There was discipline and everyone was expected to carry their weight and respect one another, but unlike the data-driven Netflix model, Shelley was looking to create a long-term relationship with her employees. She built an environment where she not only would want to work but also that worked for her employees and their families.

"I had a real authentic company. It was a family, the good, the bad, and the ugly. We didn't hide the truth; we shared truths and then we worked our way through them," Shelley says.

With Shelley as the CEO, OTX thrived. But this model is not the culture celebrated in a start-up world where words like "lean" and "efficiency" are most admired. One of the issues is that companies want absolute loyalty—but there's no reciprocity. At the media start-up, I spent months hiring an entire team only to be fired the week my team started. That, sadly, is the new relationship. We are in an age where industries are contracting and evolving, and qualified people are being laid off, forced out, or simply fired.

The paradigm of the workforce is shifting. It's like we are all on corporate Tinder swiping right, maybe getting laid, and then moving on to look for something better. There's no long-term marriage, just a series of flings—and if you're lucky, an occasional short-term relationship. If this is the new normal, how do we protect ourselves? What can we do to succeed?

BE READY TO REINVENT YOURSELF AGAIN AND AGAIN

Deb Copaken texts me that she's running a few minutes late. The express A train has gone local and it's taking forever to travel the 150 blocks or so uptown to her stop in Inwood, at the upper tip of Manhattan's West Side. She's making the pilgrimage from a guitar shop downtown, where she was getting guitars restrung for her kids: Jacob, twenty, Sasha, eighteen, and Leo, eight. Deb plays the guitar too, though she has never taken a lesson. She taught herself the chords by watching YouTube, and now she can hack her way through just about any song and on occasion performs in New York, singing and strumming.

Perhaps Deb's approach to music is a metaphor for her creative, bold, and fierce DIY spirit. Deb is fearless and frank, smart, provocative, and unabashed. Her petite frame is almost at odds with her piercing blue eyes, which make her seem bigger and stronger. Deb says she is the "master of making shit work." She is undeniably a woman who makes things happen for herself often, and often against the odds. Deb has reinvented herself multiple times because she's wanted to and because she's had to. This is why for weeks I have been stalking Deb, trying to secure an interview time amidst her overstuffed schedule. And it's why on a Sunday night, the last day of the school winter break, I'm sitting with Deb in her cozy kitchen. She is offering me tea and dried apricots while she makes Annie's Mac and Cheese for her youngest child Leo. Her older two are away in college.

Earlier today, she had dropped off her daughter at the airport. Sasha was heading back to Northwestern University, where she's a freshman. As we talk, Deb gets a call from Sasha to say that she landed safely in Chicago and is wondering if her birth control arrived at her dorm. Deb assures Sasha that it should have been delivered and to check the mail room. She describes the six-month odyssey of getting birth control coverage for her eighteen-year-old daughter. It's fitting that we are talking about the obstacles women face in both securing birth control and getting insurance coverage. After all, sexism, sex, and health insurance are topics Deb frequently dissects in her writing. But Deb may be best known for her 2000 *New York Times* best seller *Shutterbabe: Adventures in Love and War*. It wasn't a book about sex, but rather a memoir about her experience as a Paris-based war photographer fresh out of Harvard, covering conflicts in Afghanistan, Haiti, Russia, and Zimbabwe in the late 1980s.

Shutterbabe was an intimate look at Deb's adventures, capturing history and war through the camera lens in a pre-Internet, pre-cell phone, pre-ISIS world. Her memoir details her hustle, grit, and spicy sex life during this time. The book also grapples with the sexism she faced and the realities of being a young menstruating woman near the front lines. In one of *Shutterbabe*'s opening scenes, Deb gets her period in the back of a truck as she's embedded with the Mujahideen—the freedom fighters in Afghanistan.

The tampon stash she's toting in her backpack gets soaked and explodes. She's left bleeding on the side of the road, with only makeshift sanitary supplies.

Shutterbabe was both lauded and excoriated by the media, Deb reminds me. She shows me a review of the book that ran in *Talk* magazine that still horrifies her. In a few snarky sentences, the article, written by a female reporter, manages to reduce Deb to a self-aggrandizing, narcissistic, bored mom whose writing ability is questionable. And even worse, the biting description slut-shames Deb and implies that a date rape on the eve of her college graduation was something that maybe, possibly she brought on herself. At the end of *Shutterbabe*, Deb writes about choosing motherhood over hopscotching around the world covering war-torn nations. This turn in her story causes another reviewer, this time a man, to proclaim Deb a feminist sellout. Slut and sellout—she can't seem to win. The reviews stung then, and even in their half-life, continue to sting.

"When the reviews for *Shutterbabe* came out, it was the first time that I was in a fetal ball on my bed thinking that the world is mean to women who are trying to succeed," Deb says. "It's particularly mean to mothers who try to succeed and particularly mean to women in nontraditional roles who are trying to succeed."

But *Shutterbabe* is Deb's baby, even though she never liked the title. She is proud of the memoir and the positive and empowering impact it's had on her female readers, who still write to her frequently. Deb says that she wanted to call the memoir *Newswhore*. The term is used in news circles—not about sex, but about journalists' near vulture-like obsession with getting the story. Playing on the double entendre, Deb also wanted to reclaim the word "whore" in a way that, years later, Lena Dunham would successfully do with *Girls* on HBO. But Deb's publisher pushed back and *Shutterbabe* stuck. All these years later, the "babe" still makes Deb cringe.

Living Out Loud, Loudly

In many ways, the book still defines Deb, but she truly defies any definition. Memoir writing is just one of her accomplishments. When I ask Deb how she describes herself these days, she goes into the living room and grabs a business card and then looks at her Facebook profile on her iPhone. Depending on the audience or the gig she's trying to land, she's a combination of an artist, an author, a storyteller, a photographer, a screenwriter, and a performer. Deb lives out loud and lives loudly. She doesn't fit neatly into any box, as so many of us don't. And that's partly why I am here. In fact, I would not have known about all the ups, downs, pivots, and somersaults Deb has experienced, except for the fact that she has broadcast them. She has no fear of speaking up, even if it's not the polite thing to do—especially if it's not the polite thing to do. In 2013, Deb wrote a piece for *The Nation* about sexism in the literary world that her friends warned could blow up her writing career forever.[6] She took the chance. Deb says that because of this nuclear piece, she most likely will never get another book deal for a novel or memoir from a traditional publisher. She believes that she has offended the publishing establishment and has burned too many bridges. But she has no regrets.

I knew Deb from her post-war, pre-*Shutterbabe* days when she was an associate producer at *Dateline NBC*. Even then, she had a big reputation: former war photographer and current badass. She was also married and a mom to two small children. In August 1997, when Princess Diana was killed in a paparazzi chase, Deb was on a six-month unpaid maternity leave with her newborn daughter. She got a call from the executive producer of *Dateline* to fly to London because he knew that she knew the photographers who were arrested. Deb was still nursing every few hours. Her daughter was not weaned, but she got on the plane, forgetting her breast pump. She was squeezing her boobs across the Atlantic to extract her milk. Not long after the Diana story, Deb decided that the news life was too unpredictable and not compatible with raising small children. She had friends who were making hefty advances on their book deals, and she had always envisioned a novel or memoir about her experience as a war photographer. So she gave it a shot. Within a few months, Deb sold Random House a proposal for what became *Shutterbabe*, for twice her *Dateline* salary.

Over the past decade or so, I've tangentially followed Deb's career. I've seen her appearances on the *Today* show when she was promoting new books or discussing articles she wrote about parenting. I've read about Deb in several *New York Times* columns showcasing her life, from her eclectic social circles to her then-pioneering move to Harlem. I've read articles that she's written for other publications. And then seemingly out of nowhere, in November 2014, Deb's post from the women's website Cafe.com, "How I Got Rejected from a Job at The Container Store," appeared on my Facebook newsfeed. The piece was raw and poignant and completely unexpected. It left me and others flummoxed. How did this happen to Deb Copaken? In social media language, the messages went something like: OMG, WTF, seriously?

It's All Personal

The piece was about Deb's failed attempt to get a job as a greeter at The Container Store over the holidays. Having just been fired from her position as an editor at a health and wellness website, recently diagnosed with breast cancer, and needing health insurance for herself and her kids, Deb was understandably desperate. It all began with what looked like a spam email from The Container Store advertising holiday employment with benefits. The benefits piece especially intrigued Deb. She applied for the holiday greeter gig, was rejected, and as many writers do when they have personally powerful fodder, she shared her story with the world.

It began:

"Last year, during a ten-month period, the following happened in this exact order: I got separated from my husband of two decades, who, having lost his job to the recession, moved across the country to start a business, leaving me as sole provider and parent to our two children still at home; I abandoned the novel I was working on and found a job with benefits as an Executive Editor at a health and wellness website; I took a boarder into the room newly abandoned by my college freshman to help pay my rent, which the new owners had hiked up an extra $900 a month because they could; I was diagnosed with stage 0 breast cancer; I watched my company, which was preparing to go public, fire dozens of qualified people within my first month of work, after which I was informed that my job, too, was on the chopping block; I survived the cancer but was fired from my job. Then, unable to afford my rent any longer, I moved my remaining family into smaller digs."[7]

The piece went on to describe the details of Deb losing her health insurance and the COBRA nightmare that ensured. And then she drove the point home—a point that made headlines, stirred controversy, and had the TV networks calling.

"Because seriously, if an Emmy-award-winning, *New York Times* bestselling author and Harvard grad cannot land a job as a greeter at The Container Store—or anywhere else for that matter, hard as I tried—we are all doomed."

The story went viral. Many saw themselves in it. With an economy in flux, no one is safe; we are all vulnerable. The story was also radioactive. Some called Deb whiny and entitled. If she really wants a job at The Container Store, she should scrub her Harvard pedigree from the resume, others suggested. And why should an Emmy-award-winning producer be expected to get a retail job at The Container Store anyway?[8]

Amidst the snark and schadenfreude, many others related to the piece and had compassion for a newly separated mom of three struggling to keep it all together, managing a health crisis, and paying her bills. The piece resonated with me too, deeply. I've lost my job, been fired from jobs, and searched for more jobs than I can count. I've responded to jobs online and applied for many positions that I was overqualified for. Hustling for work and stressing about money is never far from my mind either.

Deb's piece wasn't simple clickbait; it was intended to spark and drive conversation. She was speaking her truth, her reality. And Deb's reality was that while she had just landed a new position as a writer at Cafe.com, the website that posted The Container Store piece, Deb's job was only paying her $34,000 a year as a full-time writer. That salary for New York City was unconscionably low, even by low-paying blog-writing standards. But Deb accepted the position because she had MRIs, breast cancer follow-up appointments, and doctor visits for her kids. Her plan was to take this gig and supplement the salary with other freelance work.

"I thought I could do eight hundred other jobs. It was about getting my foot in the door. It was about getting the health insurance," Deb says.

The piece proved strategic. It hit the second week into her job at Cafe.com and immediately Deb got a raise. "I think they realized they were going to lose me if they didn't give me a decent salary and that it was going to be really bad press for them if anyone asked me what I earned and I said $34,000," Deb says. "Later I found out a guy exactly in my position was earning $200,000 a year. He was an editor and a writer like me. So immediately I got a raise to $80,000, which was still pathetic. I kept saying, 'I can't make it on this salary. I can't make it.'"

But Deb is the definition of hustle. She's not whining; she's working her ass off.

The Master of Making Shit Work

"Last year, I would wake up at four in the morning and write my books or my screenplays, and then I would do an eight- or nine-hour day at work, and then I would come home and feed the kids and get my daughter's college applications done, and then it's nine at night and I'm doing other stuff like editing photos that I shot," Deb says. "Sometimes I would sneak out of work to do extra jobs. I literally snuck out of work during lunch and said that I was going on a two-hour lunch. But I did a photo shoot for a friend that I edited that night. And for my vacation, I got a gig for *Good* magazine to go to Paris. That way I could take my child on vacation someplace cool and get paid $5,000 to do that. I'm the master of making shit work."

Within a year of The Container Store piece running, Deb was fired. Her boss told her that they were taking a different tack at Cafe.com, which was renamed Mid.com, before they bought and merged with Scary Mommy, a site with a different tone and audience. He also said that they couldn't afford her, even though she was still making well under $100,000 a year.

"You're expensive, my boss told me," Deb says. Her boss was apparently self-funding the venture, using family money. When the company started looking for investors, her salary, though still small by New York standards, was large by online writing standards, and it stood out amidst other salaries on the balance sheets.

I tell Deb that something similar had recently happened to me at a company populated by Millennials whose salary was a third of mine because, well, they had a third of my experience.

"Corporate America is screwing its seasoned workers. And they are using the excuse of expense. I don't know what the answer to all of this is," Deb says.

The answer may be to have lots of jobs and keep multiple options open. Deb says in 2015 she had six major jobs. She had a full-time writing/editing job at Cafe.com. She was a freelance photographer and writer. She wrote the screenplay for *Shutterbabe*, after it had been in the hands of many others over many years. She also sold three books: *The ABCs of Adulthood, The ABCs of Parenthood*, and *The ABCs of Love*. And in a more corporate move, Deb also landed a position as the Vice President Deputy Editorial Director for Health at Edelman, a communications agency.

"In 2016, if you don't do seven things, you don't survive," Deb says. "You have to learn how to be a hybrid. Whatever you've learned, whatever your skillset is, you have to learn another one... and maybe another," Deb says. "All of us are capable of doing anything, except for things like brain surgery. You need to really study for that. But basic life skills and basic creative skills are attainable by anybody. And we are in an amazing age for that because we can learn it all on YouTube or Google it."

To prove her point, Deb walks me into her living room where a large, beautiful canvas hangs above her sofa.

"I just painted this," Deb tells me, smiling.

Inspired by a recent Frank Stella exhibition, Deb wanted to see how he created art with masking tape. So she went onto YouTube and saw that she needed to buy a particular gel. Then she realized that she didn't need a frame if she painted the sides, so she made a point of remembering to paint the sides.

"I don't think that innate intelligence is important. I think that for all of us, no matter the level of our intelligence, whatever our IQ, it's just a matter of saying to yourself, 'I am capable of doing anything, I just have to learn how,'" Deb says.

Like the rest of us, Deb can feel stuck and even bitter. But it doesn't stop her from looking forward and figuring out what she needs to do to move ahead. A piece to this puzzle is staying relevant by showing your relevance. In a social media world, optics is everything. Putting yourself out there is essential these days. It's not about ego as much as it is about seeking more opportunities and staying top of mind for others.

"As far as promoting myself, I get shit for it. It's subtle. I'll be at a dinner party and people will be like, oh yeah, you're on that Facebook all of the time," Deb says. "I'll be like, that's what I need to do to keep my career alive. You cannot *not* be on social media these days. You cannot *not* be a brand these days. You have to be your own mini-mogul because nobody will be it for you."

Getting Younger

Two months after interviewing Deb, I see on Facebook that she's taking a two-week leave from her job at Edelman to join the TV show *Younger* as a writer/consultant in Los Angeles. The show is about Liza, a forty-year-old divorced mom of a teenaged daughter who suddenly needs to get a job after her ex-husband leaves her financially ruined. Liza realizes that reentering the workforce at forty is crazy hard, so she decides that to get a job she's going to fake being younger—much younger. Liza's best friend gives her a makeover and she pretends to be twenty-six years old. Goodbye forty, hello twentysomething! Now faking youth, Liza bubbles with confidence and lands a job as an assistant to an editor at a publishing house. It's the quintessential modern girl relaunch sitcom.

Funny enough, when I tell people about this book that I'm writing, several people suggest that I watch *Younger*. So the fact that Deb landed a writing gig with the show working with the acclaimed executive producer Darren Star feels like serendipity, or karma, or that it obviously is just meant to be. Except that we know from chapter 3 that it's not just a happy accident Deb got this job. She had forces in place to help make this happen. She is at the helm of engineering her own serendipity.

Deb says that she and Darren Star have known each other since 2001, when he bought the rights to *Shutterbabe* for Dreamworks. They went on a trip to Paris together for research, became friends, and have remained friends ever since.

"We were having dinner recently, and he was asking me all sorts of questions about what a divorced middle-aged woman would think and do. I was telling him funny stories about dating younger men, and he just asked me to write for the show," Deb says.

Deb is about creating, evolving, and figuring it out as she goes. This strategy not only fulfills a passion, it pays the bills. She understands the need to stay nimble and adapt to change. As she says, we are living at a time when we can learn just about everything we need from research on Google or YouTube. But we can also learn new skills from online classes, through workshops, at universities, or even leaning on mentors or others in our networks. Rather than feeling stuck or irrelevant, it's empowering to know that we can keep evolving, well beyond what we may have initially trained to do. In fact, it's important that we make this happen.

As we will continue to learn in the next chapter, staying relevant, being top of mind, and keeping your options open is critical to marrying timing with opportunity.

7

FLIPPING OFF FAILURE

"It is impossible to live without failing at something, unless you
live so cautiously that you might as well not have lived at all, in
which case you have failed by default."

—J.K. ROWLING

"**IF YOU HAVEN'T FAILED YET,** you haven't tried anything,"
Reshma Saujani, forty, tells me matter-of-factly as we sit
in a small, nondescript conference room in New York at
the Girls Who Code office, where she is the founder and CEO.
Reshma knows what it's like to fail, and to fail publicly. In 2010,
at thirty-three years old, Reshma ran in the Democratic primary
in New York City, making headlines as the first Indian-American
woman to run for a Congressional seat. Passionate, whip-smart,
and camera-ready, Reshma raised money, got good press, and
won support from influencers in New York's business and tech
world but ultimately lost in a landslide to the popular incumbent,
Congresswoman Carolyn Maloney. "It was humiliating," Reshma
says. "I felt like I let people down."

Reshma hangs her feelings of failure out there for all to inhabit. It's a slice of her story that has teachable moments, but
Reshma is no cautionary tale. While she embraces failure as part
of her journey, grit and determination are arguably the more

potent pieces. After all, this is a woman who applied to Yale Law School three times before getting accepted. Not surprisingly, the fear of failing didn't stop Reshma from rebounding—in this case, running again for office. Three years later, after serving in the appointed position of New York City Deputy Public Advocate, Reshma ran for Public Advocate. She lost that race too. The fact that things don't come easily for Reshma doesn't deter her. In fact, it's part of her narrative. She expects an uphill battle, and like her role model Hillary Clinton, she is prepared to fight the good, hard fight.

THREE TIMES IS THE CHARM

"I never get things the first time or the second time—more like the third or the fourth time," Reshma says. In fact, it was Hillary Clinton's concession speech in the 2008 Presidential election that inspired Reshma to leave her job on Wall Street as a hedge fund lawyer and first run for Congress. Reshma says that when Hillary was addressing thousands of supporters in Washington, DC, she felt like Hillary was speaking directly to her.

"It would break my heart if, in falling short of my goal, I in any way discouraged any of you from pursuing yours," Hillary Clinton had told the cheering crowd. "Always aim high, care deeply about what you believe in, and when you stumble, keep faith, and when you're knocked down, get right back up and never listen to anyone who says that you can't or shouldn't go on."[1]

The words resonated.

"She said just because I failed doesn't mean you shouldn't try," Reshma says.

Despite the pollsters' bleak odds for Reshma winning the Congressional seat in 2010, she went for it anyway. She desperately wanted to serve. The daughter of political refugees expelled from Uganda by dictator Idi Amin in 1972, Reshma grew up in Illinois, painfully aware of the need for social justice and cultural diversity. With a master's degree in public policy from Harvard and a law degree from Yale, Reshma has the pedigree for politics and from an early age was leading movements to increase diversity awareness. She says that she led her first march when she was twelve years old.

While losing races was miserable, what she saw on the campaign trail—the lack of girls with access to computer science classes in New York City public schools—sparked a passion in Reshma. What had begun as a campaign promise to increase computer science education became the nonprofit Girls Who Code, which Reshma launched in 2012. Its mission is to close the gender gap in technology. With help from Google, Twitter, Microsoft, and Facebook, Girls Who Code provides free computer science education to low-income girls across the country. Its ambitious goal is to get one million girls coding by 2020. "If you asked me ten years ago if I would be a nonprofit leader, I would say absolutely not. It was not something that I had aspired to do," Reshma says. "If you asked me if I would be running an organization that would be closing the gender gap in computer science, I would have probably laughed because I'm not a coder. In many ways, it was the other choices I made that didn't work out that led me to this place."

And getting to this place was not easy.

"After I lost my first Congressional race, I bounded upwards. I was looking for what the next opportunity was," Reshma says. "But after losing Public Advocate, that was pretty painful. I did everything I wanted to do, and I had the right narrative, and I just didn't win. I was like, damn, maybe I'm just not electable. Maybe there isn't another race."

Recovering from Failure

The political was also personal and the campaign took a brutal toll. Reshma wasn't only running a campaign, she was also trying to get pregnant. She had two miscarriages during her run for Public Advocate and suffered another miscarriage earlier. "One of the things that kept me going was I didn't want to get lost in my own grief and get broken," Reshma says. "When you fail, you can become broken and never recuperate, and I think that's what women are afraid of. What if I try this and it doesn't work out, and what if I never recover?"

Now the mom to a ten-month-old son, Shaan, Reshma is keenly self-aware and reflective about how she handles and processes both failure and recovery. She's learned it's the picking yourself back up that keeps you going. "That fear of never being able to recover makes some women not try at all. I practice recovery. I now know that if something bad happens to me, what I need to do for myself is to recover and move on. I know that failure won't break me," she says. Reshma even has a protocol for grieving after a failure. She has rituals. People often ask her how she handled losing two elections and applying to Yale Law School three times. "We go to India to this ashram and drink a lot of booze and complain and go over every little thing that happened, what I could have done differently," Reshma says. "It's three months and then I'm done, and I don't move back into the past. I think giving yourself a finite time to grieve and to mourn and then to pick yourself up and move forward is really important."

Don't Teach Perfect, Teach Brave

Reshma is no doubt charging forward. She has been recognized as one of *Fortune's* "40 Under 40" and has earned accolades as one of *Wall Street Journal's* "Innovators" and one of *Adweek's* "Young

Influentials." And in February 2016, Reshma gave a TED Talk about how we need to teach girls to be brave and take risks, rather than be perfect. Reshma's experience running for office inspired her book, *Women Who Don't Wait in Line: Break the Mold, Lead the Way*. The book speaks about the importance of embracing risk and failure and how women need sponsors—people who can help women rise through the ranks. Reshma says she was shocked by the reaction she received from many women during her Congressional race who were upset that she would dare run against another woman. "The idea of waiting your turn and waiting for the big welcome mat—I believe this is what holds women back," Reshma says. "The fact that I decided I wanted to run rather than someone tapping me to run is what leads women to not ask for raises, and to not take double steps in their careers, and to not take risks."

It's a Mindset, Not a Skillset

Taking risks and showing resilience and grit is what Reshma believes is fundamental for women and for the next generation of girls. Success, she believes, is less about skill and more about mindset. "I've been a lawyer, a candidate, I've worked in government, I'm a nonprofit leader—I've done fifty thousand different kinds of things, and I don't have the training to do any of those things," Reshma says. "I didn't go to a school to launch a nonprofit or school to become a candidate. I think having a mindset that you can do anything and step up to any challenge, along with the fake-it-until-you-make-it idea, is really important."

Reshma says that her failures got her to where she is today. Running for office prepared her to run a business. Enduring scrutiny helped her to develop even tougher skin. "There is nothing more frightening than being a candidate," Reshma says. "You are being judged by all the things that we as women hate. You have to talk about yourself and brag about yourself and convince people to vote for you. And you get beat up every day."

Now Reshma's mission is supporting other women. She says that sponsorship is the new feminism. We owe it to each other to pull each other up. "Our generation is different because I don't feel like we believe that there is only one spot for one woman," Reshma says. "I don't think we are as competitive with one another, because we feel like there is plenty of room for all of us. We have to be unabashed about supporting other women and be generous about opening up our networks to them."

Like Amina Sow and her Tech LadyMafia in chapter 3 and Rachel Sklar with Change the Ratio and TheLi.st in chapter 4, Reshma sees the importance of lifting women, sharing her network of contacts, and women actively encouraging one another. In essence, our collective future hinges on our supporting the sisterhood. Having flipped failure on its head, Reshma describes Girls Who Code as being "like unicorns and rainbows." She says that she's seen the best parts of humanity in people coalescing to help girls. After her failed battles for public office, you may think that Reshma would be surprised that she has successfully landed, but she's not.

"Sometimes success is easy. I'm used to fighting for things, but this has not been one of those things," Reshma says. "It wasn't novel; it was really obvious and there were other people who were in the space. Sometimes it's the right idea at the right time."

But if timing is everything (or at least a chunk of it), perhaps Reshma landed exactly where she needed to be at just the right moment. It wasn't magical. She saw a need, had a passion to help solve the problem, built an organization, and had the support of influential members of the tech community—a community she had cultivated when she was running for office. Reshma wanted to effect change, and she's doing it. "I'm unique in the nonprofit space because I'm impatient," Reshma says. "I want to move fast."

WEB THERAPY

Bea Arthur, thirty-one, is a charismatic African American woman with a name she calls a "happy accident." She wasn't named for the actress of *Golden Girls* and *Maude* fame, but for her father's professor who coincidentally resembled the American TV star. "I tell people that the woman I was named after was actually a tall, mannish white woman," she says with a laugh. Bea embraces the association with the other Bea Arthur because, living in New York City's Chelsea area (with its population of gay men known for adoring the *Golden Girls*), she says she is asked about her name all day, every day. "I love it. I'm like an old cranky Jewish woman from Miami on the inside," Bea says.

But this Bea Arthur comes off as anything but cranky. People are immediately attracted to her huge smile and contagious energy. Born in Houston and one of five kids, Bea says she inherited her entrepreneurial spirit from her parents. Bea's father has a PhD in public health and was the head of immunization for the City of Houston's health department. He recently retired and bought a cassava farm in Ghana to create an import/export business in glucose syrup. Bea's mom started a personal health care business when Bea was in seventh grade. They now have twelve personal care homes in the Houston area.

Bea earned a dual master's degree from Columbia University in counseling and clinical psychology and is a licensed mental health counselor. To qualify for a license, she spent nearly five years slogging away in Medicaid centers working with drug addicts, which she found exhausting. Then Bea moved to FEGS Center for Women and Families in its domestic violence division. She loved the work and the dynamic of working with all women. It was there that Bea realized that therapy should be accessible, affordable, and anonymous for everyone: "I figured all of our other dirty secrets are on the Internet, why not therapy? People are always so curious about therapy and want to try it, but there is always so much stigma. I thought: Let's have fun with the stigma."

Bea's vision was to make therapy something empowering and even preventative. Don't wait until you're in crisis to get healthy; make it part of your routine. She had read about a place in Japan where you go and buy ceramic plates and cups and then break them to relieve stress. They clean them up and you leave. Bea loved that concept and wanted to create an environment where therapy was invigorating—you get it out of your system, find relief, and carry on. Regular sessions would keep you balanced and healthy, like going to the gym. And making it personal, affordable, and easy to access was the key. "Therapy is seen as something for weak people, but I wanted it to be a powerful thing," Bea says. "I wanted to create a monthly model, like a gym membership. I stay away from the term mental health—it sounds too much like mental illness. People think therapy is for people with too many problems or too few problems, but there is a huge middle."

Play Dates Gone Bust

This was Bea's second attempt at a business. A few years earlier, while she was babysitting to make extra money, Bea realized that many of the stay-at-home moms she met (former high-flying career women) were suddenly lonely and eager for adult conversation. This led Bea to create Me Too, a space on the Upper East Side for women to have "adult play dates" while their children were occupied with childcare in the same brownstone. Bea found an investor to support her business, but her timing was off. It was 2007, and the economy was collapsing. The well-to-do at-home moms who were paying Bea's $500 monthly fees were exactly the ones whose husbands were losing their jobs in the financial industry. The cost of renting a brownstone was not sustainable, and within three months Bea's business fell apart.

"I hadn't told anyone about it. I was super-secretive. When it failed, I was lonely and depressed. I should have seen a therapist, but I didn't want to because I was in so much credit card debt," Bea says.

The irony struck her. As a therapist, she couldn't afford the help she needed. "I'm a practitioner in the space, and I thought how much harder it must be for the average person who couldn't afford therapy even if they wanted to," Bea says.

Pretty Padded Room

Bea's experience inspired Pretty Padded Room, an online destination to find and receive therapy that is accessible and affordable for everyone. In February 2011, while still working at FEGS Center for Women and Families, Bea launched the company with five other therapists. They each had a specialty, their own distinctive "superpower," as she calls it. Bea was targeting Millennials and created a concept she thought was cheeky and inviting. Even the name, Pretty Padded Room, played with the stigma of therapy. The idea was that you could first get to know the therapists by watching videos about them. It would be personal and easy. She wanted to show that therapy wasn't just for those in acute crisis, but could also be helpful for everyone during life transitions.

They started with free sessions and immediately got some great press. But Bea couldn't afford to quit her day job. She was working during the day and would go to Brooklyn each night to write copy and wireframe her site. She says that she became skilled and strategic at driving her own press because she couldn't pay anyone to do it for her. Bea also mastered the power of networking and leveraging other women's social feeds. "I learned how to piggyback on other people's audiences and to get other people to vouch for you," Bea says. "If it's in line with their brand and mission and it's not a direct competitor, it just makes sense."

Bea was a therapist, not a coder. She had never worked at a tech company and had no experience with building websites. But she quickly realized that her counseling business was rooted in technology, and she needed to learn the tools of the tech world. "I never thought about it as being a start-up," Bea says. "I grew up with entrepreneurs, so I just thought I was running a counseling company. But it turned out that I was running a tech platform with no experience in programming and no team and a broken site. Our video didn't work for the first fourteen months, but I knew that we had something because people were trying to sign up."

Swimming with the Sharks

Bea was also hustling for money and investors. She appeared on ABC's *Shark Tank* in 2013, hoping to get funding for Pretty Padded Room. The reality TV show experience was demoralizing. Bea says the day she taped it remains one of the worst days of her life.

"Being on that show was like walking down an alley and getting jumped," Bea says. "Nothing can prepare you for that level of personal attacks. It was surreal. Imagine five people criticizing the most important business meeting of your life. They asked me if I went to college. It was relentless. They had to work hard to be that mean. After I taped the show, if I was awake or alone, I was crying." Bea didn't get the Sharks' backing, but the feedback from the show forced her to figure out what her business was lacking.

Two years later, Bea was accepted into the prestigious Y Combinator program in Silicon Valley. Bea was not only the first African American woman, but also one of the few women to join this exclusive boys club, an elite accelerator boot camp known for churning out the next big tech company. Silicon Valley was another shock. While it was a tremendous entrepreneurial journey for Bea, it also highlighted the enormous gender chasm that exists in the tech world when it comes to being taken seriously and raising money. Bea found that gender, not color, was the bigger barrier to entry.

"If you're a black guy, they think, that's cool. With women they just see this as a lifestyle company. It's crazy because 98 percent of start-ups fail, so you are defending this discrimination on a formula that isn't even working," Bea says. "Ever since I entered the realm of investors, it's really pissed me off. I'm from Texas; my family is from Ghana. I'm from two very patriarchal cultures, and I've never felt as dismissed and as discriminated against as a woman since I've been on the start-up scene. And then there's the sexual harassment. There are a lot of games, and people don't take you seriously. They think, 'Keep it up girl, you're really scrappy, good for you.' I've hustled for every dime of the half million I have raised."

Three months with Y Combinator during the summer of 2014 gave Bea the tools to truly develop her business. She learned to think differently about how to scale and grow her company. The program teaches you to work toward where you want to grow, and hire and behave as if you're leveling up. You operate from a place of power—a very alpha mentality. While at Y Combinator, Bea renamed her company to In Your Corner. Men, she says, never related to the ironically named Pretty Padded Room.

In February 2015, Bea had her official relaunch with the new name. The experience was overwhelmingly stressful. A couple of bad hires resulted in her wasting money and time. Her website wasn't functioning properly. She was losing momentum and faith from investors. She was also losing her mind. "I was powerless over my own products," Bea says. "It was a purgatory of panic attacks, and there was nothing I could do about it. There is a lot of talk about depression in the start-up space. There's a lot of pressure.

You are paying attention to false rewards and getting caught up in the attention and excitement."

Bea's blunt honestly is refreshing. The fairy-tale of the successful start-up dominates the media. While the stories of twenty-something founders with quirky ideas that turn into massive payoffs are what we hear, the reality is often much more bleak. The struggles that founders face are daunting; add being a woman in the tech space and it's even a tougher climb.

As a coach and therapist, Bea often shares advice and the lessons she's learned with other women about how to create their own businesses and take leaps forward.

"You have to be aggressive, shameless, and fearless if you want to start your own company," Bea says. "You can't be scared of being embarrassed. You can't be scared of failing."

Sometimes You Can't Beat the Odds

A year after we first talk, Bea posts a heartfelt message on her Facebook page. She announces that after five exhilarating and exhausting years, she's taking down In Your Corner. The company is folding. I can feel every ounce of Bea's emotion wrapped up in her poignant post. She's been profiled as the glamorous "Beyoncé of Tech" for *Forbes*, exalted in *ELLE* magazine as a "Woman in Tech to Watch," and in *Fast Company* as "The Comeback Kid." She has spoken on panels, at conferences, and on TV. Bea even appeared in The Limited's fall 2015 apparel campaign about innovative women. And yet, the odds of creating a sustainable start-up are still stacked against her. Despite turning a profit, year after year, Bea can't get the funding she needs to keep her business going.

Bea and I meet two weeks after she posted her Facebook message.

"I'm sitting shiva," Bea says with a smile, using the term for the

Jewish period of mourning. She seesaws between being light-hearted and feeling like her heart is being ripped out. When Bea was in San Francisco the summer of 2014 after she completed Y Combinator, a well-known female investor and founder invited her to brunch in her palatial backyard in Palo Alto. Bea was excited; she had just finished the program and was eager for advice from a female mentor. Instead, she got a warning. "I really like you, but it's not going to work out for you here," Bea says the woman told her. "You can't do the big-dick swagger and be cocky about your revenue. You're non-technical, you're black, you're a woman, you have a really cute name, your company has a cute name. It's just not going to work out."

Sadly, Bea feels there was truth to those words. The odds of any start-up succeeding are remote—but for a woman in tech, the obstacles are staggering. They often can't raise the money they need. Ironically, they aren't taken as seriously as the boys in their hoodies. The gender discrimination is well known and pervasive.

A 2015 study published by CraigConnects (an organization created by Craigslist founder Craig Newmark to use tech to empower under-recognized groups) and Women Who Tech (whose goal is to promote women-led start-ups) found that only 7 percent of venture capital money goes to women-led start-ups, even though women bring a 35 percent higher return on investment when venture-backed than male-run start-ups. Another interesting nugget: Female entrepreneurs bring in 20 percent more revenue with 50 percent less invested. And yet, women can't get the funding that they need.[2]

As we eat lunch, Bea's phone beeps with text messages. She has job offers. Some of the most connected people in tech are reaching out to her. But she doesn't know if she wants to be someone else's employee—at least no time soon. Bea wants to stay true to her passion and mission of helping others. She still believes that therapy is something that should be available to everyone, whether through a mobile, digital, or good old-fashioned in-person experience.

"Failure is like a redirect for the universe," Bea says. "I did way more than I ever thought I would accomplish when I was at FEGS making $38,000 a year as a domestic violence counselor. Over the past few weeks, it's felt like my heart was gasping for air, but I know there are lots of good things on the horizon."

THE FAILURE FETISH

Embracing failure is an idea that has become fetishized in Silicon Valley. With an estimated nine out of ten start-ups flaming out within a few years, failure is as universal to the Valley experience as relentless optimism. Believing that they are working on the next big thing that will transform the world keeps those in the start-up space grinding away, even if the staggering odds of success are against them. But that is the beauty of the culture of innovation. An environment that encourages risk ultimately creates change.[3]

Failure wasn't always so fashionable. The tech world used to bury its dead without much fanfare. Companies folded quietly. Founders whose businesses flopped got rescued and hired by friends. But then something changed. In 2009, Cassandra Phillipps, an event production planner who had entered the start-up scene in San Francisco, grew tired of pretending that everything with her social media business was perfect. She launched Fail-Con, an event where entrepreneurs could share their stories of epic fails, the lessons they learned, and the emotional roller coaster they experienced. This was Cassandra's way of making it real—ripping off the façade of the founder myth that everything was fabulous.

Cassandra had felt that wherever she went, people would boast about their successes and talk about how great things were going and how pleased their investors were with their company's growth. But that wasn't Cassandra's experience. Her company was floundering. She was depressed. She longed for support. "I would go to the events and everyone was so positive, and I felt like I had to do the same thing or I would be kicked out of the community," Cassandra says. "It felt like you were a failure if you were having problems. You couldn't ever be honest about how you were doing. It made me feel like personally I was a failure. I wondered why everyone around me was doing so well. I felt like we couldn't discuss it in this environment." So she changed the environment.

The FailCon event was a safe space to share what went wrong. When it launched in 2009, it was a huge success, with nearly five hundred people at the inaugural event. It quickly grew to more than twenty events around the world. Now the once-quiet funerals of start-ups have loud platforms where people can publicly mourn and broadcast their experiences. It became trendy for entrepreneurs to post their postmortems on blogging platforms like Medium with essays like "First Start-Up. First Flop." Some even saw it as strategic, announcing their failure as a way to look for another job. It's like advertising: "Hey, I did all of this great stuff, but it didn't work out. I'm seasoned, I failed, hire me!"

Fail Fast + Fail Forward

Aside from owning failure as a professional bragging right, the "fail fast" mantra is often cited as a popular business technique of the tech industry. The idea is that many products aren't fully baked before prototypes are released to the public. Think Gmail: It was released internally to Google employees in 2007 and then released to the public a few years later. These are known as the beta versions. The tech world is obsessed with speed and getting first to market. The expectation is that nothing you initially launch is perfect—it doesn't need to be. It's not about perfection; it's about acting quickly. Companies try out products for people to test. What sticks they keep, what doesn't they toss. It's a learning experience. They improve on features, they tweak, they iterate, they adjust, just so.[4]

This model—risk, act, fail, and iterate—is equally useful to our careers. Many psychologists will point to experiencing failure as a valuable step in the journey to success. It's a critical learning tool, because it forces you to dig into your own reservoir of grit. It tests your perseverance and ultimately can make you stronger. "Failure really *can* be an asset if we are trying to improve, learn, or do something new. It's the feature that precedes nearly all successes. There's nothing shameful about being wrong, about changing course. Each time it happens we have new options. Problems become opportunities," writes Ryan Holiday, author of *The Obstacle Is the Way: The Timeless Art of Turning Trials into Triumph.*[5]

Talk to anyone in the midst of failure, and they'll say it's messy and awful. There is plenty of pushback now about how glorifying failure masks the horrible reality of the toll a tanking company takes on its founders. But for women, there is something to be learned from the start-up culture that takes the stigma out of failing and encourages risk—confidence. In chapter 2, we discussed how the proven way to gain confidence is to take action. Even in failure, you've acted. You've taken risks. You've learned. And out of failure comes growth. "We've come to see the theory of failing fast as the ideal paradigm for building female confidence," write Kitty Kay and Claire Shipman in *The Confidence Code.* "If we can embrace failure as forward progress, then we can spend time on the other critical confidence skill: mastery."[6]

DEVELOP A GROWTH MINDSET

Both Reshma and Bea have what best-selling author and Stanford professor Dr. Carol Dweck would call a "growth mindset." As the name suggests, growth mindset states that intelligence and learning aren't fixed but instead are malleable and can develop. This growth mindset versus fixed mindset has become very trendy in progressive education and parenting circles over the past decade. A cousin to iteration, it's also been embraced as an integral part of the start-up world. And experts argue that it can predict an entrepreneur's ability to succeed or fail. Fixed mindsets see failure as lack of innate ability—it means you're not smart or talented and you're not fulfilling your potential. Failure makes the fixed mindset person fearful of taking risks, whereas people with a growth mindset don't measure their failures by their own fixed traits. They bounce back more easily. They recognize the value in what they learned, even if they failed. They are more resilient. They see success as a combination of luck with hard work and persistence. And they see failure as having teachable moments. "The number one ingredient in creative achievement is having a growth mindset," writes Dr. Dweck in her best-selling book *Mindset: The New Psychology of Success.*[7]

Dr. Dweck had long been obsessed with how people cope with failure when she started doing research on children many years ago and found that some kids really stepped up their game when they were challenged, while others did not. In her book, Dweck shows how her findings on dealing with failure can help parents raise kids by rewarding grit and perseverance. And the byproduct of those traits, not surprisingly, is confidence. The view you embrace, Dweck argues, profoundly effects how you lead your life.[8]

Reshma Saujani's failures didn't hold her back; they pushed her forward. As Reshma says, no one taught her how to run a campaign, to be a candidate, or to be the leader of a nonprofit. She tried, failed, tried again, learned, and grew. And this is the recipe for success. It's the risk-taking that leads to growth that leads to success. Some people are more intuitively programmed to embrace the growth mindset, while others need to actively adopt the approach. Not winning political office didn't stop Reshma from pursuing a mission to close the computer science gender gap. She lost her quest for political office, but she moved forward by creating a meaningful nonprofit that is changing the lives of thousands of girls across the country. Arguably, in her position today, Reshma may be making more of a difference than if she had won political races.

Two weeks after shutting down her company, Bea Arthur isn't exactly sure of what she will do next. But she too has the growth mindset of someone who won't become paralyzed because her company didn't survive. She swam with the sharks on *Shark Tank*, rebounded, launched a company against the odds, and positively impacted people's lives with her therapy site. Bea knows that her passion for connecting and helping people will still be part of her future. She believes in the strength of who she is and knows her capabilities and also what she doesn't do as well. "No one can fire you from your gift," Bea says. "Nobody can fail or not fund your gift. I was made for this. I do believe I have these gifts, and I feel very, very strongly about that."

8

ITERATE. MEDITATE.
REPEAT.

"What you are is what you have been. What you'll be is what
you do now."

—BUDDHA

NAAMA BLOOM IS APOLOGIZING FOR the blender. We are
sitting in the café of her communal office space, WeWork
in New York City, where two bearded hipsters sporting
nearly identical geek chic eyewear are whipping up smoothies.
WeWork is like a kibbutz of cool kids, a collective of entrepreneurs who run small companies and start-ups in a shared office
space custom-made for the creative economy. It's among the
bean bag chairs and foosball tables where anyone from the solo
publicist to the nonprofit activist to the software engineer can
meet and collaborate. Naama, forty-two, a lanky brunette in jeans
and a funky peasant top, fits right in. She points to the tiny nose
ring she got herself for Mother's Day this year. "Getting to forty
is like fuck you. It's liberating," Naama says. "I got my nose pierced
for Mother's Day because I always wanted to get my nose pierced.
No one is not going to hire me because of a nose piercing. I've
proven myself."

ROCKING THE AD INDUSTRY

Naama has definitely proven herself. In July 2013, she launched HelloFlo, a subscription company that sends "period kits" filled with tampons, sanitary napkins, candy, and other little treats— basically, custom-care packages for your menstrual period. She introduced the world to HelloFlo with arguably the greatest video to ever kick-start a company. The cheeky "Camp Gyno" video, viewed more than twelve million times, shows a precocious tween girl at sleepaway camp who acts like the know-it-all when it comes to girls getting their periods. The edgy script used the word "vag" and proclaimed that getting the HelloFlo candy-filled packages felt like Christmas at camp.

"It was the beginning of summer, and no one knew me at camp," the girl begins. "I was a just a big random loser. Then things changed. I got my period. The red badge of courage!"

As the sudden expert on the topic, this little camper becomes the insufferable "camp gyno," hosting graphic "menstruation demonstrations," barking orders through a bullhorn at fellow campers, and bullying those not in the know. "For these camp-ers, I was their Joan of Arc," she says. "It's like, I'm Joan, and their vag is the ark." But the camp gyno loses her power because Hello-Flo arrives in the bunk. It's a lovely package with tampons, panty liners, and candy that dethrones the Queen Bee.

"All perfectly timed to their cycle! It's like Santa for your va-gina!" the girl cries, flopping down on her bed in defeat.

"Goodbye Camp Gyno. HelloFlo," reads the text on-screen.[1]

The "Camp Gyno" video went viral, and within days of launch-ing in July 2013, HelloFlo and Naama were in the news. It was declared by many in the industry as the best ad of the year and won numerous awards. And it firmly planted HelloFlo on the map as a game-changer in how girls and women talk about their monthly periods. Adios blue liquid feminine product ads! HelloFlo!

A year later, in June 2014, Naama released another video, "The First Moon Party." This stars another sassy tween—but this time the issue is that the girl hasn't gotten her period yet when all of her friends have. So she decides to fake it to fit in. She paints a pad with red sparkle nail polish and proudly shows her mom. Her mom knows that she's lying but plays along and throws her daughter an embarrassing "First Moon Party" to celebrate her arrival into womanhood. Grandpa arrives along with mom's co-workers to play Pin the Pad on the Period. There's also bobbing for ovaries, a vagina cake, and a "vagician."

"Do you know how hard it is to find a uterus piñata?" the mom asks at one point.

The video is clever, silly, and smart. When it came out, my eleven-year-old daughter Lexi watched "The First Moon Party" at least a dozen times. She was obsessed. And that's exactly the audience Naama hoped to reach. It demystified getting your period. The video made it real, celebratory, and funny all at once. Together, the "Camp Gyno" and "First Moon Party" videos have garnered more than fifty million views on YouTube.[2]

Goodbye Amex, HelloFlo!

Things haven't always lined up seemingly so easily for Naama. For nine years, she worked in marketing at American Express. The last four years there she was in a rut. Even though Naama was getting top reviews and bonuses, she couldn't move up the corporate ladder. She was passed over for two digital marketing positions. Right around her nine-year mark at the company, Naama got pregnant with her second child. During her maternity leave, she started networking with as many people as possible to explore other job options. Friends thought she was nuts for "wasting" her maternity leave, but it made her feel reenergized about working.

"I kept getting feedback at Amex, like you need to be more like this or more like that," Naama says. "It felt like the culture was asking me to change my personality."

Instead of changing herself, Naama left American Express and took a new marketing job at a tech start-up. That's where I met her—I was doing freelance publicity, and Naama was my client. After a meeting one day, Naama mentioned she was trying to launch HelloFlo on the side out of her Brooklyn apartment and asked for my feedback. Would girls dig this? Would moms want this? "Absolutely!" I told Naama. My friends' daughters were all on the cusp of puberty and were consumed by getting their period and the mystery of when it would happen.

Two years later, I was thrilled for Naama when the "Camp Gyno" video exploded online. The company was born out of the premise that mail-order subscription services can be successful. Modeled after Birchbox and Harry's Shave Club, Naama envisioned creating a company that could fill a niche in the marketplace for women and girls. "It kind of started as a game," Naama says. "My friend and I were both working for other people and not happy. We were moms of two young kids with full-time jobs and thought that none of these current subscription companies work for us. So we had an idea of monthly care packages for moms from sex toys to other stuff, but everything we came up with seemed like too much of a luxury. The problem we were trying to solve is that moms take care of themselves last. We were walking down the street, and I thought, what do I have to buy each month? And that's when I came up with the tampon idea."

Naama's friend was not enthusiastic about a feminine hygiene business, but Naama couldn't get it out of her head. She kept talking to her friends about it. "My husband said, 'You either have to do it or shut up, but it will drive you crazy if someone else does it and you don't.' And that shook me into action," Naama says. "I didn't put any money into it. I figured in the beginning it wouldn't be more than one hundred people ordering kits, and I could go to Costco and buy stuff, pack boxes in my apartment, and ship them. I thought it would take a while to grow, and while it was scaling up I would figure out what I would do."

The first move was launching a video. The "Camp Gyno" video emerged out of a conversation Naama had over a Thai food dinner in her apartment with a friend and her boyfriend, an advertising copywriter. Naama knew her target audience was ten- to thirteen-year-old girls and their moms. She shared her insight that every girl has a friend who knows more than she does. Naama also talked about her own experience at sleepaway camp, where there was always one girl who seemed to know everything. The ad agency writer immediately said, "She's like the camp gyno. The girl who gets her period first is the educator and gets out of control."

The video was born. Calling in favors from friends, cameramen, and editors, Naama paid only $6,000 to have "Camp Gyno" shot and edited. The boldness of the video hit a nerve. Immediately, the response from girls and their mothers was overwhelming. "I got thousands of emails from women around the world, and it made me realize that this is not just a subscription business, but a new way to talk to women about their health. It's a new conversation."

Moving from Kits to Content

The concept for HelloFlo quickly pivoted. "I originally thought I was building a product company, but what I ended up building was a marketing channel and a content business," Naama says. HelloFlo still sells period starter packages, teen kits, new mom packages, and other supplies cheekily described as "one-of-a-kind kits for your lady bits." But the company evolved quickly, becoming a rich platform for smart, bold content for tweens, teens, and adult women, covering female bodies from menstruation to menopause. The HelloFlo site contains all types of period-related topics and also what it calls "feminspiration," sitting at the intersection of inspiration and feminism.

As a marketing guru, Naama knew how to talk to her customers to find out what resonates. After the "Camp Gyno" video hit, she took the cues from the girls and women who wrote to her and tweaked her business to reflect what she saw as the real need in the market. This is also where she excelled at—creating a marketing channel steeped in smart content. "What was interesting for me in this big aha moment was that you start out doing one thing, but what you end up doing is what you're naturally really inclined to do and what you're good at," Naama says. "I wound up doing what I was always good at instead of what I was trying to do."

Naama had never intended for HelloFlo to be her full-time gig. She had envisioned it as a part-time business with consulting on the side. Little did she realize that it quickly would become more than a full-time job, but without the salary. "I figured when it was full-time, it would pay me full-time money. I didn't realize that there is such a huge gap between one and the other," Naama says.

Naama was shocked that after the wild success of her videos, she still couldn't raise venture capital money for her company. And the popularity of the videos didn't translate into massive subscriptions for the kits, either. While she was getting recognized in the advertising and media world for her compelling content, she was drained by the unrelenting stress of running a small business and operating with a razor-thin margin for error. Her husband David, also an entrepreneur, was trying to grow his start-up too. As two entrepreneurs with two small kids in Brooklyn and mounting debt, it was overwhelming. So in 2015, Naama was thinking of an exit strategy. She had pivoted HelloFlo from a commerce company to a media company. Now she needed a partner.

Reframing the Business and Finding the Right Fit

Naama had been nominated for the annual #Femvertizing Award that SheKnows, a women's digital media company, gives to brands that show women in a positive light. SheKnows's President and Chief Marketing and Revenue Officer Samantha Skey is also a Brooklyn mom with two young kids. Samantha reached out to Naama to meet for coffee. As Naama says, it was an instant and mutual girl crush. "I got excited about all the stuff we could do together and over the course of that coffee, I even said to her, 'You guys should really just buy me.' We talked about where the holes and opportunities were in what SheKnows was doing, and it fit perfectly with what I know how to do."

Naama left the coffee date feeling pumped. She called her husband to say that maybe it would turn into something. Still, she knew that these first meetings often feel promising but usually go nowhere—as she says, a lot has to go right. But Naama had a brand that was valuable and aligned perfectly with SheKnows, and she also had a personal skillset that filled a need for the company. And perhaps most importantly, Naama had a very motivated internal sponsor in Samantha Skey. "I realize after observing friends trying to go through acquisitions that you need a very senior-level corporate sponsor internally," Naama says. "Everyone has competing interests inside an organization and so much work to do that it's easy to not let something happen."

In March 2016 (three and a half years after Naama launched HelloFlo), SheKnows Media acquired the company, giving it a much larger home. Naama also got a new job title as Senior Vice

President of Integrated Marketing for SheKnows. Six months earlier, Naama had landed a contract to write a nonfiction book about puberty. The week I spoke to Naama, she also told me how thrilled she was to be invited to the White House State of Women Summit. After years of packing tampons into boxes in a small shared office space and hustling for deals, Naama feels like she now has validation. Ironically, it's not from the start-up tech world in which she initially imagined the roots of her business, but instead from old-line companies in traditional publishing and media that have given her a sense of internal worth. "I really felt rejected by the tech and venture community. I couldn't raise money, and I felt like no one ever got me there. It felt like the establishment in the start-up world was never accepting of me, and I think I bought into that," Naama says. "But all of a sudden the establishment in the book publishing world, and now the White House invitation and SheKnows, is acknowledging that I did do something sound. And I think, oh yeah, I did do something! It is worthwhile."

Naama struggled to be understood by the tech community and raise capital for her business. After an initial fundraising hustle, she stopped trying. But not only did Naama pivot her business, she also reframed what her business was and what she wanted it to be. And when Naama did that, it started feeling more authentic to her. It made sense. She's not getting invited to elite Silicon Valley events, but she's going to a women's conference at the White House. She's been acquired by a women's media company—a space in which she clearly belongs.

"At a certain point, I stopped defining my industry as start-up and tech because when I was defining myself as that I felt like I was failing," Naama says. "I didn't have a fast scaling start-up that raised a ton of money. Once I realized that I'm not a commerce company and I started saying, 'I'm a women's health company because I talk about women's health, sell products around women's health, and do education around women's health,' it started making a lot more sense to me, and it was more true to me."

Naama realized she couldn't shoehorn herself into a tech community that didn't connect with her, and equally as important, she couldn't relate to them. "The start-up world idolizes twenty-six-year-old boys who, granted, know how to build stuff, but that's not my world," Naama says. "I don't want to say there is no room for women in that world or for forty-plus-year-old women, but it's definitely less open to women and people over forty. I just realized, why I am competing in this level? I don't want to compete with these people. They're not my people. I also don't want to run a business that doesn't make money. What is so great about these start-up businesses if they don't make money? Business should make money, that's the whole point."

HURRY UP AND SLOW DOWN

Three thousand miles across the country, Suze Yalof Schwartz wants to make money too. When she first opened her doors at Unplug Meditation in 2014, she gave away meditation classes for free—a flawed pricing model, she admits. But she's come a long way. When I sit with Suze in a spartan, white concrete room in Santa Monica, California, next to her chic meditation studio, there is no need to give anything away. Down the hall, pink and violet lights bring calm to a packed room full of people practicing the wildly trendy art of meditation in Unplug's signature class. Young moms sporting tats mingle with middle-aged men who will be putting on suits and heading to work after thirty minutes of organized mindfulness.

Suze, forty-seven and a mother of three boys, is dressed head to toe in black—still clinging to her New York City DNA, where she lived for twenty-one years. Even after three years in the land of kale and cutoffs, a February wardrobe still means black. Suze says she had a dreamy job in New York where she was an executive fashion editor for *Glamour* and before that worked for *Vogue, ELLE,* and *Marie Claire.* A media darling with a sparkling smile and infectious energy, Suze's specialty was the makeover. She regularly appeared on *Good Morning America, CBS This Morning, The View,* and the *Today* show to work her magic. Suze did everything from transforming a rabbi into what she called "synagogue chic" to making everyday ladies more glam. A fashion editor, director, and stylist, Suze was touted as "the fairy godmother of makeovers" by *the New York Times.* And then on a whim (or more like a dare), her husband Marc, who always had a hankering to live in L.A., encouraged Suze to be adventurous and move West with him. He landed a new job and found the house and the school for the kids, and in August of 2012 they packed up and headed for the Left Coast.

For Suze, who had always worked full-time, the move left her unmoored. Life in the mommy bubble of kids' activities, home decorating, and school stuff made her restless and bored. So she began commuting back and forth to New York, working for Lord & Taylor where she taped commercials that appeared in New York City taxicabs. With three young children at home, however, the bicoastal commuting took its toll. She was stressed and unhappy. Suze's mother-in-law, a psychotherapist, recommended meditation. Suze was intrigued. But every type of meditation she found was expensive and inconvenient. She could either take a four-week trek to a Buddhist temple or commit to an eight-week series of sessions that cost more than a mortgage payment.

Suze realized that accessibility and affordability could transform a mindful and emotional experience that would benefit everyone. So Suze sought to reinvent meditation for the masses and give a makeover to a 2,500-year-old monastic practice. Tapping into what she saw as an emerging interest in mainstream meditation and her own desire to meditate, Suze envisioned a

Drybar for meditation—a nod to the inexpensive blowout hair salons where you can walk in and, for a reasonable fee, leave feeling fabulous. She also wanted to model Unplug after the wildly popular SoulCycle spin studio business, based on drop-in classes with no monthly membership required. "Honestly, it started out as a selfish venture," Suze says. "I knew that I needed meditation the most, and I couldn't find any place that looked clean and smelled clean and where you could just conveniently drop in when you wanted to."

Leaning on friends with business experience, Suze cobbled together a rough business plan. She didn't have a business degree, but she had a deep bench of contacts and bartered her own skills for the help she needed. "I used my career as currency," Suze says, explaining that she gave closet makeovers or media training to people who could help her, from a graphic designer to an accountant. "I was bartering with everybody. People would say, 'How can I help you?' People want to help their friends. When you have a friend who has a dream, you want to help her."

Suze's former life helped her in other ways too. She edited and curated every detail of the studio space, including the way classes would be run and how instructors would speak to the participants. She wanted to stay away from the "woo woo" stuff often associated with meditation and instead get straight to the point. The goal was to design a secular, inclusive, affordable version of meditation that resonated with the cool kids and even the guys in suits. At Unplug, there is no incense or sitting cross-legged required. People sit on comfortable sleek black chairs or lie on mats. Suze's slogan is "Hurry Up and Slow Down."

The Spiritual Entrepreneur

Today, Suze calls herself a "spiritual entrepreneur." She still misses Fashion Week in New York but is thrilled by what she is building with Unplug. As it evolves, the business is becoming something that she had not predicted. "When I started Unplug, I kept thinking SoulCycle for chic, stressed-out mommies," Suze says. "But it's a really rich experience and so much more. It's evolving into what is a really cool dinner party. You meet people who are not in your social circle. They're from really different backgrounds and have really different stories, and that makes it so interesting."

Since Suze opened Unplug, meditation studios have sprung up in New York City and other parts of the country. As someone who spent a career in fashion as a trend spotter and stylist, perhaps it's no surprise that in Suze's move into mediation, she would also be on the cusp of a trend. "I really do I feel like I was hired to be the PR director of meditation," Suze says. "Did I start meditation? No, but I was the one who started the ad campaign for meditation. It's amazing. It was nowhere and now it's everywhere."

Unplug has evolved since it opened its doors in 2014. It now has more than five thousand people coming each month to find focus, reenergize, and reduce stress, including mindful media mogul Arianna Huffington and new-age guru Deepak Chopra. Suze says that one of the smartest things she's done is put a black lucite suggestion box on the front desk. It's the old-school feedback approach, but fitting, given how her mindful meditation business is the antidote to our angsty modernity. Suze says she gets about fifty suggestions a week, from what types of classes to offer to how to make the bathrooms more Zen-like to cell phone policies. "I hear from my customers, which is better than any meeting we could have. They look at my website and give great feedback, and I think, because of them, we are what we are," Suze says.

Suze is also surprised by how much of her former life in fashion has managed to creep into what she does today. She loves buying merchandise for the store portion of her studio and picking out every doorknob and fixture. She also sees the most unlikely parallels between the rhythm of fashion and meditation. "I've been surprised by how limitless this business is and how much it's like fashion," Suze says. "It changes every day and it never gets old. Meditation is always a surprise; it's totally unpredictable—you will never have two meditations that are the same."

Mindfulness as a Business Strategy

As Unplug expands, Suze sees new outlets and opportunities to bring meditation online and to corporate America. While the ancient root of meditation came from ascetics, not capitalists, Suze has found that the corporate world is gravitating toward mindfulness as a business strategy. Music mogul, entrepreneur, and yogi Russell Simmons is bullish on meditation and thinks everyone in Hollywood and business should practice the art of being centered and focused.[3] At the Milken Institute's Global Conference in 2016, Simmons said, "Money doesn't make you happy, but happy makes you money."[4] Corporate America seems to be listening. Unplug has brought teachers to the Wharton school of business. They've held classes for McDonalds, Deutsche Bank, Chipotle, and the NFL.

"I'm not a thinker, I'm a doer," Suze says. "I jumped in feet first and I didn't think too much about how I would build this. I learned as I went along about what works and what doesn't. I was a C student. I'm not a brain surgeon, but I have big ideas. When you really focus on the steps to achieve your goals, you can do it, and so what if you fail at first? You learn and adapt as you go."

When your business is rooted in meditation, an added benefit is its residual byproducts of calm and focus. And for a woman who tends to be guided by instincts and passion rather than business strategy, Suze has found the perfect muse in her mediation business. "I'm calmer now. I can redirect my emotions from a more mindful place," Suze says. "Before I make decisions now, my feelings are so crystal clear."

TAKE ACTION:
LET PASSION LEAD YOU FORWARD

Suze had no experience in business or expertise in meditation, but followed a passion and used her contacts and aesthetic sensibility to drive a vision forward. She spent time learning about meditation and talking to people about how they launched their businesses. She leaned on her contacts for both business help and for media attention. She tapped into her core talents and even bartered her skills of media training and style makeovers to get the help she needed to launch her business. She wasn't afraid to act. She believes that all of us can pursue our dreams—we just need to act. "You can do two things at the same time," Suze says. "You can work for your company and write your business plan. You don't have to quit your job while you work on your big idea. Take the time to invest in yourself. Wake up an hour earlier and go to bed an hour later. We can all lose one hour of sleep. Just do it and stop talking about it. You don't want to live your life looking back and saying, 'I should have tried that.' Make it happen."

Naama didn't want to look back and regret, either. She too acted and leaned into what she knew well, which for her was strong content and marketing savvy. She also iterated. She talked to potential customers. She even asked me what I thought about her business. Did she strike gold with her video? Absolutely. Having a viral video to launch a business is like winning the lottery. But her success came from taking a concept that had not been done before and speaking in an authentic way to an audience who was ready for it. The important first step for Naama was taking the initiative to leave her company to pursue an idea. "AmEx wasn't working for me anymore, and I was banging my head against the wall," Naama says. "You have to listen to those cues. If that feedback feels like it's asking you to change who you are, listen to that and internalize it. Three years later, I release two viral videos and am on *Ad Age*'s 'Creativity 50 List.' You don't always have to change; sometimes it means you need to change companies."

Neither Naama nor Suze had expertise in the business arenas that they were launching, but both had a passion to take an untapped idea to the public. They both had to pivot their initial business ideas to grow. They had to adapt to their audiences. They used their contacts as currency to get noticed. For Naama, it was calling in all the favors she could to get that first video produced, largely for free. Suze used her media contacts to get stories written about Unplug. They both successfully tapped into their natural skillsets and applied them to growing their businesses.

They went all in.

Many women may not want to ask others for help or insight or even to barter like Suze does. But the sharing of resources may be exactly what you need to push your project forward and transform an idea into something real. "I have been a sharer," says Suze. "I'm happy to give it all away, why hoard? Helping someone makes me feel good." And all of that sharing has come back to Suze. When she needed it, people were there to help her. Amina Sow talks about sharing her network a part of who she is in chapter 3, and Suze operates in a similar way. The lessons from Naama and Suze are relevant to anyone launching a business, whether online or brick-and-mortar. Listen to your customers. Use the feedback to adapt and iterate what you're selling. Lean on your contacts and barter resources. Leverage your own talents and skillsets, and remember that your strengths are transferable. And as we discussed in chapter 2, it's about confidence—it's the doing that leads you forward.

9

THE MOTHERS OF REINVENTION

"Do one thing every day that scares you."

—ELEANOR ROOSEVELT

T'S NINETY-NINE DEGREES IN SCOTTSDALE, Arizona, and several hundred women toting Dove-branded swag bags stuffed with products ranging from gluten-free granola bars to branded zip drives are meandering around the patio at the Ritz-Carlton. Sprinklers are spritzing water to make the midday desert temperatures slightly more bearable, as a group of women in flip-flops compare notes on the best way to get companies to pay for their video content.

This is the seventh annual Mom 2.0 Summit, a conference that writer Laura Mayes conceived with Carrie Pacini in 2008 as a place to bring moms and marketers together while the blogosphere was maturing and online brand marketing was exploding. "Mom Influencers" were gaining currency with marketers, and companies like Procter & Gamble and Disney wanted to tap into them to leverage their reach. The more than six hundred women attending this year's conference are mostly "content creators," social media mavens, entrepreneurs, and marketers. The term "blogger" and its pejorative relative, the "mommy blogger" (a term I was once called when I blogged about work-life balance for several sites), have evolved. The majority of personal blog sites don't get much direct traffic today because most people find their "content"—the catchall for everything from an article to a video to an Instagram post—directly on social feeds like Facebook. And yet, because of the Facebook amplification effect, the bloggers' audiences continue to grow and have reach.

When Mom 2.0 first launched there were few true digital natives, women who had been weaned on tech. Instead, the women who initially attended Mom 2.0 and similar conferences like BlogHer were Gen X early adapters who created blogs and their video sisters, vlogs. These women cultivated devoted online audiences as they shared their candid, irreverent, and sometimes snarky tales of motherhood. According to Mashable, in the golden age of blogging around 2012, there were nearly four million "mom blogs," but only about five hundred women had cut through the online chatter and had large enough followings to be considered *influencers*—the women with the clout brands coveted.[1]

The bloggers spanned the country, and their voices and backgrounds varied. In 2011, *the New York Times* christened Heather Armstrong, a liberal ex-Mormon who lived in Salt Lake City, as "Queen of the Mommy Bloggers." Her successful blog Dooce.com, where she originally wrote under the pseudonym Dooce, would become blogger lore—at one point attracting one hundred thousand daily visitors and earning more than a million dollars a year through ads. Armstrong chronicled her pregnancies, postpartum depression, and the banalities of suburban life: the Maytag washer malfunctioning, her high-maintenance dogs, and the kids' doctor visits. There was also Ree Drummond's The Pioneer Woman, where the former Los Angeles party girl who married an Oklahoma cowboy and had four kids wrote about life as a ranch wife raising cattle, making gravy, and homeschooling her children. And as far away from a cattle ranch as you could get, there was Alice Bradley of Brooklyn, with her witty and intelligent New York City fiction sensibility, creating the award-winning Finslippy blog. All three women's blogs still exist but arguably may no longer be the destination sites they once were in their heyday. They have had to change with the times.[2]

Still, the women at the Mom 2.0 conference love all that's associated with what attracted the first generation of female bloggers—the community, being on the cusp of something modern, enterprising, empowering, and yes, the potential for attention and dollars from brands. Most don't expect to turn projects into Dooce-style million-dollar businesses, but all are hoping to create new careers for themselves, often while their kids are napping.

For three days, I meet women who hail from just about everywhere (including Australia and England), and their online savvy runs the gamut. Some women are intrigued by the changing social media space and are trying to figure out if they can carve out a place in it. Many other women have small sites or online businesses they are hoping to expand. A smaller group, higher up on the food chain, has it pretty much figured out. They are the ones with book deals, speaking gigs, and corporate sponsorships. Some do national satellite media tours to promote brands and are paid $5,000 to $10,000 for a few days of work. No doubt, they are the outliers but are aspirational nonetheless.

Dove is sponsoring the event, so it's all upbeat girl energy. There are yoga classes and morning hikes and meditation. And there are seminars on everything from email marketing to pitching national media. There is also plenty of mingling and Merlot, networking and bonding. Motherhood is the thread that connects almost everyone, and all products entrepreneurs display are kid- or mom-relevant.

FROM MBA TO MOMABLES

At a cocktail party on the opening night of Mom 2.0, I meet Laura Fuentes, thirty-five. The gentle lilt in Laura's accent gives away her Spanish roots. Born in Madrid, Spain, Laura moved to California when she was twelve years old, not speaking a word of English. After college in California, Laura got her MBA at the University of New Orleans and met and married native Louisianan Eric Schneller. For several, years Laura worked in pharmaceutical sales and marketing, which she says had nothing to do with her degree in international business development. Hurricane Katrina slammed into New Orleans in 2005, devastating businesses and homes—including her husband's physical therapy business. All of the hospitals where Laura had accounts were flooded. She was the breadwinner and was now making no money. They didn't flee; they stayed to rebuild, and Laura soon discovered that she was pregnant with her first child.

"'We can live on beans and rice,' my husband told me, 'if you want to stay home,'" Laura says. "I stayed home, but within a few months I really missed what comes with work performance and achievement. I had a hard time accepting the role that I was just a mom. Then I had a second child, and within a few years I knew I had to do something creative to keep my mind occupied."

She started developing a prototype for a lunch container that would keep fresh food cold. At the same time, Laura was also writing a blog about the food fights in her kitchen as she struggled to get her young kids to eat healthy food. The blog, Supergluemom (now Laurafuentes.com) was Laura's way to keep in touch with her family in Spain and her mom in California. She would share news when she had a victory in the kitchen, posting recipes and photos of her kids eating the healthy food she prepared. Her blog gained traction. Aside from her family, others were discovering it, finding her recipes and relating to the stories she shared with them. "I was surprised that people found my homemade chicken nugget recipes interesting," Laura says. "I learned so much from all the struggles with feeding my own kids that I was able to create things that people are looking for. I didn't know the online space. I was learning with my personal blog, and that took a turn and became more recipe-oriented the more I saw people responding to the recipes."

At the same time that Laura was feeding her blog, she cashed out her retirement account to pay for the design and prototyping of her lunch container, which would later be manufactured in China. During the third round of prototypes, Laura picked up the container from an importer, a three-hour drive from where she lives. When she hit her brakes hard at a railroad crossing, the prototype flew off the front seat and broke beyond repair. Laura would not be able to test it. "I had just written this big check," Laura says. "It was like the sky had broken. I called my husband and I cried until there was no more to give, and when I finally was able to pick myself up, I said, 'I'm not meant to create a container.' My husband said, 'Drive home, it's not a big deal.' I just had a feeling that I wasn't meant to be in the product manufacturing and retail business. By the time I got home, I had this vision that I would be doing something that helped moms feel good about the food they make for their families. I thought, parents don't need another Lunchable; they need a MOMable. And that's how MOMables was born."

In late 2011, while pregnant with her "surprise" third child, Laura launched MOMables as a weekly meal plan subscription with family-friendly recipes for even the pickiest of eaters. She includes all of the items needed to make family meals possible and charges a fee for subscription. She has built an engaged community of eighty-five thousand parents and gets hundreds of emails each week from parents desperate for help on feeding their kids. She loves the feedback from the parents; it gives Laura a true feeling of purpose and personal impact.

Stay Steady and Do What You Love

In 2013, a publisher contacted Laura to write a cookbook about school lunches. The cookbook turned into a series of three cookbooks and a chance to compete on the Food Network show *Rewrapped*, to recreate snack classics. Laura was both thrilled and terrified by the opportunities. "I'm not a trained chef. I'm a mom who taught myself how to cook by following recipes," Laura says. "My second cookbook was on snacks. I didn't even grow up in a snacking culture in Europe, but it gave me the chance to ask other parents what they look for in snacks. The icing on the cake was when the Food Network asked me to audition and compete on a show. I won making a Monte Cristo waffle sandwich with a fried egg. I won being true to myself. I realize that when you are doing what you love to do, things that may be scary aren't so scary—they become opportunities."

Laura has seized on those opportunities. She regularly appears on TV segments where she cooks and shares kitchen tips. She also contributes to several online and print publications. Laura says that her past life has helped her build her new one—her MBA gave her the skills to plan the growth of her company. These days, she's looking for strategic partners to help her reach a broader audience, and just recently her husband quit his corporate job in health care to join Laura's company.

As eager as Laura is to expand MOMables, she believes that "slow and steady wins the race." The online space is incredibly competitive, but Laura believes that she can continue to grow her business to meet the evolving ways her audience consumes content. Right now, her focus is on growing her YouTube channel and increasing TV opportunities. "My goal isn't to become famous or to have people know who I am," Laura says. "My goal is to help my audience feel really good about the food they make by providing them with the tools they need to pull it off. I feel proud knowing that in a small way I've contributed to helping parents make feeding their families easier."

WOMEN EMBRACE THE CREATIVE ECONOMY

We are in the throes of the "creative economy," where anyone can make a website, build a brand, sell products, and share just about anything on a platform that reaches the entire world. Since the early 2000s, the Internet has democratized work. Online, anyone can be a writer, video producer, political commentator, artist, filmmaker, or entrepreneur. You no longer need a storefront with a lease to sell your goods, crafts, or services. You don't need a newspaper or magazine to publish your writing, or a TV or radio show to broadcast your voice. Virtually everything can be shared, traded, bought, and seen online.

Just as the washing machine and dishwasher liberated women from the drudgery and toil of all-consuming housework in the 1950s, the Internet has empowered women to create businesses and professional identities for themselves—on their own terms. It's no coincidence that motherhood triggers an entrepreneurial spirit in many women. Women who are home with their kids may finally have the mental space to explore creative endeavors or new careers. Others are driven by necessity, wanting to develop products or services that, as moms, they find lacking. Still more women, pushed out of the workforce by unforgiving jobs that just don't merge with motherhood, also turn to entrepreneurship. Crowdfunding platforms are giving entrepreneurial women a place to test their products, raise money, and get critical feedback for ideas.

For many years now, women have been founding companies and start-ups at twice the rate of men. Between 1997 and 2014, there was a 68 percent increase in women launching businesses, and nearly 30 percent of America's business owners were women.[3] The progress for minority women has been particularly swift, with business ownership skyrocketing by 265 percent since 1997, according to an Institute of Women's Policy Research report. And minorities now make up one in three female-owned businesses, up from only one in six less than two decades ago.[4] Women are innovating and producing products and services that fill gaps in the market. There are detractors, though. Some see the fact that the vast majority of these women-owned businesses have no employees other than the employer as evidence that women still can't raise the capital they need to grow their businesses as successfully as men. Still, women are out there on their own, creating.

And if there was ever a time to create and share, now is that time.

PAVING A PATH TO TODAY

When I sit down with Meredith Sinclair, she is kicking back at the Soho House in New York City, black retro Ray-Bans perched on her nose and only traces remaining of the TV makeup she had worn that morning for a live *Today* show segment. At forty-four, Meredith, bubbly and blonde, still has the effortlessly cheerful and down-home vibe of the small-town high school cheerleader she once was. Raised in Indiana, Pennsylvania (touted as the "Christmas tree capitol of the world" and birthplace of actor Jimmy Stewart), Meredith met and married her high school sweetheart, the towering six foot seven inch television producer Jon Sinclair. Meredith jokes that she and Jon are the 1980s reality version of *High School Musical.* They moved to the big city life of Chicago two decades ago when Jon landed a job in production at *Oprah.*

For the past three years, Meredith has been a regular *Today* show contributor, doing segments on the best toys and activities for kids. When I meet her, she has just wrapped up a story about ways to keep your kids entertained during this interminably long, cold winter. Meredith's journey to *Today* show segment contributor didn't happen by accident. She nurtured a passion into a strategic online presence, growing her on-camera skills and taking smart steps along the way. When Meredith's first son Maxwell was born, she decided to leave her job as an elementary school teacher and embrace the at-home mom life. Three years later, after having her second son Truman, Meredith got restless. Her brother suggested that she write a blog to stay creatively engaged. Blogging was new in 2003, and for Meredith it began as an outlet to share her experience as a young mom of two. "The only people who read my blog were my family," Meredith says.

A few months after beginning to write on the pioneer blogging platform Blogger, Meredith was at the library with her boys reading *Chicago Parent* magazine where she saw an ad for mom bloggers. The magazine was looking to start an online mom community and put out a call for mom bloggers to submit their samples. Meredith applied and got the job, creating her blog A Mom's Life. About a year later, she went to her editors and said, "You don't have anyone doing local TV. I want to do it." Meredith had only one experience on live TV at a local PBS station in Pittsburgh, where she had volunteered to help with an on-air fundraiser. She loved the rush and spontaneity of live television and saw an opportunity with *Chicago Parent* to be its face on local television. She also felt that her skills as an early education teacher were perfect training for TV.

"Being a teacher of second graders was my first live audience,"

Meredith says. "You are on stage and you have to be compelling. Their attention span is really low. So there was a thread of sameness for me—being in front of a classroom and being in front of a camera wasn't a complete departure, and it was something I was good at."

Finding Her Voice

In the dawn of blogging, blogs weren't yet businesses and blog conferences were just emerging. There were no brands or PR people trolling for talent, just women who were trying to understand the online space and create something meaningful and perhaps marketable out of the emerging platforms. Meredith gravitated toward video blogging at a time when most people weren't there yet. "I got in early and was only the expert because no one was doing it," Meredith says. "There were writers who were petrified to be on camera, and I was doing panels on video blogging. That gave me a platform and so I was considered an on-camera person."

Meredith also spent time trying to craft her writing voice and figure out her niche. She knew she couldn't be a generalist; she needed a specialty. "When I started, there weren't that many mom bloggers. And then like Minions, they started growing," Meredith says. She dabbled in fashion and trends and kid stuff, but as her two boys got older, they made it clear that they didn't want to be fodder for her writing or photographed for her blog. Much of mom-generated content connects back to their children, but Meredith's kids were off limits. It was at blogging conference BlissDom where Meredith heard Kevin Carroll, the author of *Rules of the Red River Ball*, talk about the playground and how play changed his life as a child. "There was something about the playfulness piece that zinged me," Meredith says. "This is what I did in the classroom, and I thought I could get really passionate about it."

Meredith began focusing on play as her niche and strategically funneled just about everything she wanted to talk about through the lens of play. Even if she did fashion posts, she managed to weave play into it. She became intentional about crafting a brand for herself. At the same time, Meredith was honing her on-air skills on local Chicago television doing toy and parenting segments. She was extending her platform from online to on-air. It wasn't glamorous or profitable, but it was valuable experience. "I'm shlepping all of my stuff down to studios at five in the morning and not getting paid. But it was an amazing training ground," Meredith says.

Grabbing Hold of Opportunity with Gumption

Meredith seized a new opportunity at the Mom 2.0 summit in 2013. The conference speakers included Alicia Ybarbo and Mary Ann Zoellner, *Today* show producers and authors of the best-selling parenting book *Today's Moms*. Meredith also participated, giving a five-minute talk about her passions. Before the conference ended, she was determined to introduce herself to the *Today* show producers. This was her opportunity—three years of working in local TV segments, and now she could meet producers from a national morning show, the Holy Grail for anyone in the parenting space. So on the final night at the conference cocktail party, Meredith approached the producers and told them she had ideas for story segments on concepts the *Today* show was not yet doing—but should absolutely be doing with her as the on-air contributor. Ybarbo told Meredith to email a few pitch ideas the next week.

Television show producers get a lot of women coming up to them at these types of events looking for advice or hoping to land a segment. Most women don't follow up with the persistence of

Meredith; or if they do, they may not have the polish to secure themselves on the show. But three weeks later, Meredith was booked on *Today*. "I have moments of great gumption," Meredith says. "And the biggest things I've ever gotten in my life have come from gumption, which I consider pulling up your bootstraps, puffing out your chest, and knowing you can do this. I feel like it's a force and you have to grab it. Going over to the *Today* show producers was one of those moments."

A few days after Meredith met the producers at the conference, she followed up in an email that outlined an entire script of what she could produce on the show, even starting with the opening line, "Lifestyle expert Meredith Sinclair will show you how to make back-to-school more fun for your children." She put herself into the script. Was it audacious? Absolutely. But she demonstrated a level of confidence and what she was capable of. It wasn't all bravado; Meredith had TV segments, which she shared, highlighting her talent and skillset. She had spent years doing spots on local TV and was now ready for the next step. "In so many situations we don't have anything to lose, but we are so afraid to have gumption," Meredith says. "You have to have laid some groundwork, so when you have that big moment of gumption you have something to support it. I think as women we get more and more scared to do stuff the older we get. We've had those disappointments and those failures."

When I first met Meredith in 2011 at a different mom blogger conference in Park City, Utah, she was leading panel discussions on how to shoot cool videos. Over cocktails one night, she had mentioned to me that she wanted to write a book. Lots of people say that, but most never get beyond page one of a book proposal. But Meredith now has a book deal with HarperCollins, and her first book, *Well Played: The Ultimate Guide to Awakening your Family's Playful Spirit*, was published in June 2016.

Small Steps Build Momentum

Meredith went from elementary school teacher to local Chicago mom blogger to *Today* show contributor and published author. In 2015, she also became the national spokesperson for the Toy Industry Association's Genius of Play, a nonprofit whose mission is to show the importance of play in building critical thinking, creativity, and confidence in children. Meredith will be the first to tell you that none of this happened overnight. There were long hours, strategic relationships, tons of networking, pivoting, brand building, moments of gumption, and plenty of serendipity.

Meredith thinks women need to embrace taking small actions—even incremental movements forward can produce momentum. We may want to make immediate change, but that's not always realistic.

"We're in a culture of wanting it now," Meredith says. "I think we need to be patient with ourselves. You have to give yourself room to play with lots of things before you figure out what lights you up. For some women, it might happen quickly, and I have seen people who jump into stuff. But don't be afraid to take the baby steps. They are beneficial and teach you what you're doing right and what you want to change. If I hadn't done three years of local TV at five in the morning when no one was watching, there is no way I would've been confident to pitch *Today* show producers."

For most of us, it can be unsettling and even stressful when you don't know which way to turn or what to do next. You may be trying to move into a new position and create a project or a business, and nothing seems to be moving forward. You feel stagnant. Inertia can make you tense. The stars are not aligning, and you feel helpless. But Meredith believes we need to make peace with that in-between unsettled, unnerving space.

"The uncomfortable pauses where you think nothing is happening is often where things are brewing," Meredith says. "If we can get friendly with a little of bit of discomfort and the process, then it's not as scary. I wanted to know where I was going and see the light in my path. But you have to give stuff a minute to let it noodle. We get too afraid of those unclear places and don't realize that they're a valuable piece of the pie. It would take a lot of fear out of people if they understood that this time is valuable, even if there is no final product yet."

GETTING COMFORTABLE IN THE UNCOMFORTABLE

The U.S. Navy SEALs have a saying: "Get comfortable being uncomfortable." It applies not only to the intense and extreme physical conditions they endure, but to the psychological ones too. Lisa Skeete Tatum, CEO and founder of the start-up Landit, a LinkedIn type of career platform for women, would agree with the SEALs' mantra and with Meredith's philosophy. "Being a CEO is incredibly uncomfortable," Lisa tells me. She wakes up at 2:30 a.m. anxious about everything that needs to be done to grow her business. But Lisa believes that women need to figure out how to live in that uncomfortable zone. "That's how you learn and grow the most," she says. Most entrepreneurs share similar feelings of unease—it's often panic laced with exhilaration. When you are comfortable, you get complacent. When you are uncomfortable, you push yourself. And in those moments of discomfort, we can also develop more confidence, which in Meredith's case turned into gumption that she used to take a leap into national TV.

Meredith forged her own path to get to the *Today* show. Interestingly, she used the digital world to launch a traditional TV career. Meredith was not a brand or marketing expert and yet she figured out how to craft a brand for herself. She networked and went to the mom blogger and women's conferences that helped inform what she was doing. She volunteered for speaking roles at the conferences to increase her visibility. She met a book agent through her blogger network. She seized on the opportunity to approach the *Today* show producers and, like we discussed in chapter 3, Meredith engineered serendipity in that moment. She had laid the groundwork, saw the possibilities, and went for it. In 2015, when Meredith became the spokesperson for Genius of Play, she happily took the position as a way to give more gravitas to the platform she had been building for herself. She now travels to Washington, DC, as one of the play industry's spokespeople.

Laura Fuentes also stepped out of her comfort zone. Writing cookbooks and competing on a Food Network show with chefs tested her confidence. After the prototype for Laura's food container broke in her car, she knew her business wouldn't be a packaging product but rather an online recipe subscription site for parents that inspired community and conversation. Laura and Meredith both grew their brands and created their own serendipity-building networks, taking risks, and seizing opportunities. They even took baby steps along the way and pivoted their original plans.

After twenty years in Chicago, Meredith is moving to Los Angeles because of her husband's job. She doesn't think she will be a TV play spokesperson forever, or even beyond another five years. But she imagines at some point maybe opening play spaces for children, or a toy store, or even a play-inspired preschool. Like the "adjacent possible" described by Steven Johnson in chapter 3 as a kind of shadow future and a map of all the ways the present can reinvent itself, Meredith is laying a foundation for herself where doors can lead to more doors. "I think about how I'm going to evolve from where I am now," Meredith says. "I'm not going to be doing toy segments when I'm fifty-two years old. I don't want to be that person. I don't know what it is that I'll be doing, but I want to always be relevant to myself."

10

BRANDING IS NOT BRAGGING

"In order to be irreplaceable one must always be different."

—COCO CHANEL

T'S NO COINCIDENCE THAT I find Lyss Stern, forty-two, chilling in the "relaxation room" at the Elizabeth Arden Red Door Spa on Fifth Avenue in New York City. She had posted on Instagram a few hours earlier that she was taking a midweek "mommy time-out" and getting pampered. Swaddled in a fluffy white robe, with her dark mane piled into a messy chic bun on the top of her head, Lyss was working. She assured me that, seriously, she really *was* working. For Lyss, posting on Instagram is part of her work— it's promoting her brand and driving her lucrative luxury lifestyle event business Divalysscious Moms, or Diva Moms as it's usually called. That I locate Lyss through social media is appropriate since I had been trying to interview her about how she success-fully brands herself and her business. So about an hour after seeing the Instagram post, I'm at the Red Door Spa, perched on the edge of a leather recliner, violating the quiet room protocol, and whispering my questions to Lyss.

"I think my business has grown because mothers trust me, and my announcing on social media that I'm taking a 'mommy time-out' this morning is okay," Lyss says. "You're allowed to do these things for yourself, or you're going to go batshit fucking crazy."

GROWING DIVA MOMS WITH AUTHENTICITY

It's Lyss's authenticity and relentless self-promotion that has helped propel her business from a small company—hosting mom and kid events at FAO Schwarz and Dylan's Candy Bar—to a true direct marketing company for high-end consumer brands and New York City real estate developers. Lyss's database of nearly one million women and a robust following on social media attract companies and even Hollywood casting agents to want to work with her. Lyss tweets, posts photos, and engages with her Diva Moms every day—sometimes multiple times a day. And everything she puts out on social comes directly from Lyss. There is no surrogate or intern generating her feeds.

After graduating from Syracuse University in 1996, Lyss worked for acclaimed celebrity publicist Peggy Siegal while attending New York University at night to earn a master's in communications. Burnt out from the grind of publicity, Lyss returned to school two years later, adding another master's degree in early education. She loved the classroom, and for six years Lyss taught kindergarten and pre-kindergarten at synagogue Rodeph Sholom's day school on New York's Upper West Side. While on maternity leave with her first child Jackson in 2004, Lyss went to a "mommy lunch" and came home depressed. She was shocked by the lack of stimulating options for new mothers. When Lyss's husband Brian asked how her day was, she said, "I went to this mother's lunch and I hated it, but the good news is that I'm starting my own business."

Lyss believed she found a void in the market. She thought New York City needed trendy events for the well-heeled and well-educated mom crowd. So with three thousand dollars in retirement savings, Lyss launched Diva Moms. Today, Lyss hosts about one hundred lectures, book parties, product launches, and other events each year. She weaves her upbeat brand message into all that she does. Her Facebook, Twitter, and Instagram posts will read fabuLyss or DeLysscious, and if she loves an item, it may be included on her Lysst. She signs off with a "Big XO." Lyss realizes that the aggressive self-promotion can turn some people off. In fact, even the name of her business, Divalysscious (aptly inspired by a remark from a salesgirl at the Barney's department store), was at first rejected by her friends and family. "I remember everybody telling me, 'You can't do this,'" Lyss says. "It's kind of narcissistic, and who puts their name in the title of a company? And I said, 'Calvin Klein did it, Donna Karan did it, Marc Jacobs did it, and we're going to do it.'"

Lyss readily admits there are haters and naysayers who think she's over the top. But Lyss says her loyal followers listen. She has been cultivating her Divalysscious brand for almost a dozen years now, and when she puts something on her Lysst, women pay attention—and the product, book, or service sells. Her authenticity is everything. "I think being your true brand ambassador is most important to your brand," Lyss says. "You can't pretend to be somebody that you're not. We have a following of real moms who listen to our voice and advice."

Evolve and Adapt: Keeping Your Brand Relevant

Lyss also has an uncanny knack for sniffing out what's going to hit it big. She was the girl in middle school in the late eighties with the cool "Gear" bag, EG Smith socks, and Hot Dogger jogging suits before anyone. Her forecasting instinct is partly what makes Lyss so naturally good at what she does. "We are always in the front of the trend," Lyss says.

Before the steamy *Fifty Shades of Grey* trilogy made it to America, Lyss was already reading and promoting the erotic novels on social media. In 2011, Lyss reached out to British author E.L. James, who was selling her series through ebooks and printing on demand from a virtual publisher in Australia. Lyss offered to host a book party for James in New York. One of the Diva moms who came to the event worked as an executive at Vintage Books, part of Penguin Random House. Soon after Lyss's book party in January 2012, James wound up with a North American publishing deal.

Lyss continues to look at how she can expand her brand into products or other services for moms. She's has cowritten books including *If You Give a Mom a Martini* and has written short-form web series for NickMom and Scripps Networks. While mom events and the mom marketing world have become more crowded since Lyss first began, she believes that knowing who you are and being true to that identity is the key to growing a successful business. "It's really important for your brand to keep relevant and keep evolving and adapting and never get complacent," Lyss says. "Because of social media today, it's also easy to get caught up in what everyone else is doing, but there is space out there for everyone to be successful. My mother would always tell me, when you're at a traffic light don't envy the Porsche to your left or the Jaguar to your right—just stay in your own lane, be focused, and move ahead."

IT'S NOT ABOUT FAMOUS

Personal branding is no longer reserved for the famous and for most people, it's not about trying to become famous, either. You don't need to be a Kardashian to be intentional and thoughtful about how you present yourself to the public. And you don't need

to have a business driven on social media like Diva Moms or an email list of a million people for it to be important to develop your brand.

In her best-selling book *Leave Your Mark: Land Your Dream Job. Kill It in Your Career. Rock Social Media,* Aliza Licht writes, "Personal branding is about identifying the best version of you and striving toward achieving and communicating that every day."[1]

If anyone knows how to juice a brand it's Aliza, a communications and social media guru, who *the New York Post* once called the Yoda of the fashion industry for her nearly two decades of innovative work at Donna Karan. Aliza became a social media maven in 2009, just as brands were trying to make sense of how to engage with the public on social. Aliza created a dishy, anonymous Twitter personality, a social avatar of sorts: DKNY PR GIRL. Inspired by the TV girl drama *Gossip Girl,* DKNY PR GIRL was imagined as a filter through which Aliza could convey the world of Donna Karan. Her insider diary of the fabulous-yet-normal life of a fashion publicist became a sensation. The audience grew to 380,000 before the company decided to reveal, as exquisitely fitting to a fashion brand, a behind-the-scenes New York Fashion Week video shared on YouTube that outed Aliza. When Aliza left the company in 2015, the audience had grown to 540,000, and the company retired the Twitter personality.[2]

Repetition Is Reputation

Aliza, forty-two, embodies personal branding. While in college, she would "get dressed" when she went to class. There was no rolling out of the dorm wearing sweats and a scrunchie. Aliza loves a red lip so much that her red hair and red lips are her signature look. It's part of her personal mojo and how she presents to the world. After Aliza left her gigantic gig as Senior Vice President of Global Communications for Donna Karan, a position she still calls a dream job, she wasn't sure what she wanted to do next. "I left because there was a piece of me that was missing, and I no longer felt challenged. But I didn't have a plan," Aliza says.

The first thing Aliza did was make a list of her capabilities. When you have a job title, she says, it's very specific; but when you start thinking of what you can do, it becomes much broader than your title or the bullet points on your resume. "I was shocked to see the breadth of what I had learned in over twenty years in fashion," Aliza says. "I looked at where my strengths were within that list, but just because I knew how to do something doesn't mean I wanted to do it. So what did I actually want to do?"

Aliza realized that at her heart she was a passionate storyteller, and she became most excited when she was figuring out a brand's narrative and how it plays out in the digital space. For many women who leave big careers and are trying to reinvent themselves, Aliza says the struggle often begins with what to call themselves. "When you introduce yourself and say 'former,' you're living in the past," Aliza says. "I think you need to give people a clue as to your present and future. You also have to make it really easy for people to understand who you are and what you do."

One of Aliza's mottos is that "repetition is reputation."

"I think there is a necessity to knowing who you are, knowing how you present, and knowing what your message is—no matter what you do," Aliza says. Part of that message is being consistent. *Leave Your Mark*, the branding bible Aliza wrote the year she left Donna Karan, became an umbrella under which she could pursue other creative avenues—including her branding and digital strategy company with the same name. "I think at the end of the day, you have to pick a lane and think of a title that is almost a catchall to everything," Aliza says. "And understand that it's okay to not have it all figured out. No one has it all figured out."

EVERYONE NEEDS PR

Five years ago, Meredith Fineman, twenty-nine, quit her digital strategy job without a backup plan. Being entrepreneurial was part of her DNA. She always had side hustles, including working as a nightclub promoter while at the University of Pennsylvania. After college, Meredith had worked in Buenos Aires for the advertising agency Young & Rubicam, and as a freelance writer she was becoming well known for her lifestyle and humor blogging in Washington, DC. Meredith hadn't considered working for herself full-time as a realistic option. But as she explored what to do next, she found that whenever she tacked on "public relations" as a skillset, she would get a bite. People were interested. So in 2009, at twenty-five years old, Meredith launched her company FinePoint as a PR firm.

For three years, as she promoted everything from lifestyle to technology, Meredith started noticing how the media were growing fascinated with CEOs and founders of tech companies. They were becoming the new celebrity, with brands and platforms and growing cults of personality. This, of course, is what certain PR people can do well—craft images and position high profile people for media and industry opportunities. But Meredith didn't feel like it was fair that the benefits associated with understanding visibility and press were only reserved for those who had a budget for it. She began thinking of PR in more democratic terms. She saw it in its broadest sense as leadership and professional development skills that could and should be learned by everyone. And Meredith found that the women she met, at every stage in their career, often had difficulty talking about themselves and promoting their work. At a time when branding was everything, Meredith felt there was an enormous opportunity not only to reframe how women spoke about their work, but also to help these professional women apply strategic PR tactics to their lives.

"In 2016, talking about the work is a huge part of doing the work," Meredith says. "There's a misconception that talking about the work is not work. But it's a learned skill and it helps explain your work. With an economy that's so entrepreneurial, it's more important than ever to understand visibility and know how to be out there. My concept is about creating this projected self that you strategize around."

Go Ahead and Brag or Find Someone to do it for You

Meredith wants to take back bragging. She doesn't see it as a dirty or contentious word; instead, it's something that she feels women need to own. Meredith also believes we need the space to talk about our accomplishments and what we've done. "Women tend to verbally undercut themselves and downplay their accomplishments and give credit to someone else," Meredith says. "People don't know what you've done until you tell them, particularly if they don't know much about your industry or your job. It's a skill that is increasingly important for your career, whether you are fundraising or in a boardroom or in a classroom."

Meredith has grown FinePoint into a leadership practice with a mission of teaching women how to brag and self-promote. Successful branding has virtually nothing to do with how smart or capable you are—it's all about the public perception. Meredith says that people are rewarded by volume, not merit, and that means producing work, which today is through articles, speeches, videos, graphics, photos, or activities that highlight your specialty and superpower. This output of "work" shapes your public persona—it helps cultivate your image.

But sharing what we do and what we've achieved is uncomfortable for many women. Self-promoting makes us squeamish. Meredith wants women to get over this discomfort. She says you must get behind your work and let people know what you are doing. She advises not to use negative qualifiers when you post something, such as "This is a shameless plug for a new article I wrote." Instead, you should own the work you've done and say, "I'm really proud of this article I wrote for X. I would love it if you could share it or send me your feedback." Gracious, nice, and to the point. The goal is to have others bolster you. You want them to share on your behalf.

"When you understand visibility and why it's crucial and use PR tactics on yourself, you can help propel yourself forward and feel better about being out there," Meredith says. "Being strategic about how you present yourself is not conniving with premeditated bad intentions; it's creating opportunity to be successful."

Journalist Jessica Bennett also recognizes the importance for women to strategically bolster themselves—especially in a way that's not seen as obnoxious. In her book *Feminist Fight Club: An Office Survival Manual*, she recommends "bragging in the service of someone else" and finding a "boast bitch" to help share your awesomeness. The "boast bitch," Jessica writes, is "your female hype man. She boasts for you, you boast for her, boasting for each other makes you both look better, yet neither of you is perceived to be bragging about yourself." And research shows that having someone boast for you is effective even if it's obvious that that person is biased.[4]

MANAGING THE CAREER PIVOT

Meredith often works with people across all industries who are pivoting in their careers. They may be moving from law into venture capital, or they are entrepreneurs wanting to carve out a new image in the fashion or lifestyle space. The most immediate obstacle, as Aliza Licht would also agree, is figuring out your identity and then driving that reputation through repetition. "The biggest roadblock to visibility is not having a clear and consistent message of who you are," Meredith says. For those changing industries, Meredith suggests redoing your bio, writing pieces in publications that matter to your intended field, and creating a personal website that speaks to the new career. Meredith says that understanding how to frame yourself in the right context and knowing how visibility works in whatever ecosystem you're entering is key to raising your profile in a new industry.

Karen Shnek Lippman, who herself has pivoted from a career in public relations to one in executive search and recruiting, says a helpful tactical strategy for those trying to land a new position is to look closely at who has the position you want and to figure out where the holes in your resume are so you can get there. "Narrow down your choices and figure out what you really want to be doing next, then you work backward," Shnek Lippman says. "Go on LinkedIn, find profiles of people who match the position you envision yourself in, and look at their career paths. Read what they've written, and tailor your resume accordingly. Look at what they've done to help better fine-tune what you need to get there too. It's all out there for the taking."

GETTING A JOB: PERSONAL BRANDING 101

I'm not an HR expert, but I have spent a good portion of my career being interviewed or interviewing others. I've seen what works and what doesn't. While I used to agonize over the cover letter, online applications today mean that hiring managers don't spend much time reading them. Yes, you should have a solid opening paragraph that shows that you have knowledge or insight into the company where you are looking to work, but you don't need to be super creative or lengthy. The cover letter should be well written and not contain any spelling or grammatical errors. You don't need to sweat the cover letter as much as you should sweat your bio, resume, or portfolio (if you are asked for a portfolio).

Below is the trifecta to personal branding from the gurus: Aliza, Meredith, and Karen.

Making Your Bio Stand Out

A professional bio is something everyone needs, and it should be updated and consistent across websites and platforms, Meredith says. Your bio should easily explain who you are and what you do. Everyone needs a long, short, and two-line bio. A long bio can be a full page and can go on your personal website. A short bio is about a paragraph (and often could be the first paragraph of your long bio). A two-line bio can go under your byline or in a description if you are appearing on a panel. For the shorter versions, think of your elevator pitch and how you would describe yourself in ten to fifteen seconds. Are you an entrepreneur? A salesperson? A storyteller? Build off of that and summarize who you are in a pithy but powerful way. Have a friend or mentor read it over, because it can be extremely hard to write about yourself.

Keep current and active. Meredith also recommends updating your bio every six months to keep it fresh. Make sure to use the active voice, keeping the tone dynamic and strong. Don't use words that diminish your accomplishments. Be conscious of the language you use.

Link to the cool stuff. For any bio that appears online, link to your work if possible. If you discuss running a campaign, show the outcome. Link to articles you've written and accolades you have received. Make the bio comprehensive enough to act as a tool to showcase your accomplishments, with a link to click. If you can be booked to speak or to consult or have a course that you offer, link to that as well.

Sing and boast, but be professional. Your bio should not be simply a list of your jobs and degrees, it should spell out your accomplishments and accolades. It can contain information about passion projects and fun side projects, but it shouldn't be as casual as saying, "In her spare time, Jessica enjoys checking out the latest microbrews." Those bits of bio information are sometimes found on company websites where the tone is cheeky. But Meredith says to stay away from that kind of relaxed language. Professional bios are not a place to be playful. Also, skills like Excel or Photoshop should not be included, because they have become so common and expected.[3]

Creating an Effective Resume

Your resume is your personal marketing tool. Experts agree that you should have two or three different resumes geared toward each target audience, specific career objective, and industry you hope to pursue. You need to adapt each line depending on your goal. I have two active resumes, emphasizing different skillsets: one in PR, branding, and communication strategy and the other more editorially focused.

Cheat with LinkedIn. Karen suggests looking at the job that you want to get and see who has that position. Then see how they describe themselves on LinkedIn. What are the words they use in their summary to describe what they do? "LinkedIn profiles can be your best friend to help you fine-tune your resume, help in the job search, and cut out the noise," she says.

Be specific. Look at what the hiring manager is asking for in the specific role for which you are applying. Make sure your language matches the job description. Because of the online application process these days at most companies, hiring managers get deluged with hundreds of resumes. They may first whittle down the resumes by keywords. Making sure you have the specific words they are looking for as far as experience and skillset is the first step to getting in the door.

Find the fit. "Don't misrepresent yourself," Karen says. "Be transparent, but align your experience with the job you are applying for. Think, how do my skills and experience really line up with this job? That needs to be front and center on your resume. Hiring managers look at the first two jobs you list. Make sure they are most impactful.

Use action words. Words like "delivered," "produced," and "managed" are strong choices for explaining what you've done. You want to show your results. What did you deliver? What was the result? What kind of tangible difference did you make in your role?

Feeding Social Media

When it comes to the social media feeds, Aliza suggests keeping to a rhythm that makes sense for you. When Aliza was behind DKNY PR GIRL, she didn't have a content calendar. She posted in real time depending on what happened to her on any given day. It was the authenticity of her posts—not canned and planned, but legitimate ones—that Aliza believes helped to grow her audience. There is no magic number of tweets or posts per day or per week. But understand that what you are posting on one social feed may be very different from what you're sending out somewhere else. Different social channels have different audiences and content that work for them. Some thrive on photos or videos, others use links to articles. Staying current on what works well and how best to reach the targeted audiences is important. And because social apps like Twitter, Instagram, and Snapchat are so trendy and fluid, the rules of engagement and what works best could be outdated by the time this book is published. The good news is that everyone can become a pseudo expert on social media. Some quick Google searches on best practices and current social media trends can keep you up-to-date.

Keep it real. Genuine posts that connect back to you and your industry make sense to post. Be true to yourself.

Choose quality over quantity. Smart content with a real point of view and voice work best.

Maintain the mothership: your website. Today, everyone should have a professional website, and because of sites like branded.me and Square Space, they are shockingly easy to make. Years ago, I created a website, and I'll be honest, I did a miserable job updating it because I never learned how to do it myself. The good news is that gone are the days when you need to know HTML or have a web designer create and maintain an expensive website. I promise you, everyone can do it now, which in an entrepreneurial age is more important than ever.

Having a hub for your resume, bio, portfolio, blog, photos, videos, or anything else that showcases your work can help you sell yourself. Just having a landing page that serves as a home for your information is a great first step. It also allows you to be creative and show personality. The first thing people do when they are looking to potentially hire someone is to Google them.

By creating your own website, you are controlling the way the public will see you. And if there's one takeaway from this chapter, it's that controlling your message and owning your brand is everything.

11

GETTING BACK IN

"You have brains in your head. You have feet in your shoes. You can steer yourself in any direction you choose."

—DR. SEUSS

N OCTOBER 26, 2003, LISA Belkin wrote a controversial cover story for *the New York Times Magazine*, "The Opt-Out Revolution," about a so-called phenomenon where the most educated women in America, hitting the crux of their professional stride, were leaving the workforce to willingly and cheerfully stay home with their kids. For her article, Belkin interviewed eight high-achieving women who had all graduated from Princeton and went on to earn graduate degrees from the nation's top universities. Their husbands earned big salaries, so paying the mortgage or paying back graduate school loans, if they had any, was apparently not a concern.

"Why don't women run the world?" Belkin wrote. "Maybe it's because they don't want to."[1]

The article whipped up a ferocious maelstrom—and not just from feminists. There was backlash against the privilege of the elite and backlash against Belkin herself. There were scathing critiques about how Belkin built her argument around affluent women rather than examining the systemic issues that kept millions of moms from continuing in their careers. There was no discussion about policies like the lack of paid leave, workplace flexibility, or the medley of childcare issues that impact the majority of women in the United States. After the explosive reaction to the piece, other media followed. *60 Minutes* ran a segment where they focused on another group of uber-achieving women who were, as correspondent Leslie Stahl said, "giving up money, success, and big futures" to be full-time at-home moms.[2]

OPTING OUT: NOT REALLY A CHOICE

The narrative around opting out became framed in personal choices, ignoring the fierce societal forces and outdated workplace structure that actually pushed women out of their careers. After all, for most women it wasn't really a choice. But even if these stories stung of elitism, they resonated with women, including me. When I read the the *New York Times Magazine* piece and saw the *60 Minutes* report, I was a thirty-two-year-old mom with a toddler and an infant daughter. These stories tapped into a collective anxiety that whatever we do in motherhood, we're doing it wrong. It also fed into my fear that there was no real way to have the big career that I wanted and the precious time with my children that I craved. The conversation, not surprisingly, did not mention dads or partners or a larger corporate or cultural responsibility; the burden was on individual mothers to figure it out all by themselves.

"Perhaps the popularity of the opt-out story suggests that our country still prefers to think about family and motherhood in terms of personal values and choices and not in socioeconomic or political terms; and that to do so, many believe, would require us to adopt very un-American, European-style social policies interfering with our competitive capitalist edge," wrote Heather

Hewett in a 2005 essay "Telling It Like It Is: Rewriting the Opt-Out Narrative."[3]

I hadn't opted out; in fact, I was getting back in, taking a full-time freelance position at CNN to be a producer on its morning show, *American Morning.* The day I started at CNN was the day my daughter turned six months old and the day I stopped breast-feeding. There was no nursing room or any space to plug in privately in CNN's offices. I accepted the fact that I couldn't pump at work, and didn't feel like I had much clout as a brand-new freelancer to make waves. I was just happy to have landed a full-time (albeit freelance) position.

Coincidentally, the week I started at CNN was just days after the *Times* article came out. Not only was I not leaving the workforce, I was also writing my first book, *How She Really Does It: Secrets of Stay-at-Work Moms,* about how women take on that precarious balance of career and family. I had spent months interviewing moms about how they managed jobs and kids, while Lisa Belkin was writing about how thrilled some moms were to escape the grind. We were on seemingly opposite sides of the playground—stay-at-work-moms versus stay-at-home moms—and this rivalry was, at that moment, all the rage.

THE MOMMY WARS

There is nothing the media loves more than a catfight, and in the early 2000s we were living in the era of the "mommy wars." In October 21, 2002, *New York* magazine ran the provocative cover story "Mom vs. Mom" with an incendiary sub-headline: "It used to be the battle of the sexes: Now it's the battle of the moms. Working and nonworking mothers are slugging it out in the schoolyard over who's the better parent—and who gets to have a sex life."[4] Yikes.

New York magazine likes to stoke the fire of controversy, and here it unleashed an inferno. The piece was loaded with judgments and so-called choices and went for the jugular by challenging a woman's most vulnerable sense of self: Are you a good mother? "Motherhood, for all its well-documented joys, has become a flash point for envy, resentment, and guilt," wrote Ralph Gardner Jr.[5] The irony that a man wrote this piece was not lost on me or others. The article's photo showed the blonde stay-at-home mom in a sleeveless shirt showing off her buff, toned arms—evidence of the ample time she has to work out with her trainer. Her sex life was also steamy, though she had other challenges. "The pressure to be thin is brutal," she says in the story. In contrast, the working mom, a severe-looking brunette, wore a suit, her hair pulled tightly back, and her son on her hip looking absently away from the camera and his mother. This frosty, selfish wench-of-a-working mother, with her obvious lack of maternal connection, suggested all that was wrong with ambitious women. She was probably not putting out either.

While the article was arguably an exaggeration of the alleged aggression between at-work and at-home moms in the urban jungle of New York City, it continued to reinforce the damaging yet made-for-TV drama of the mommy wars. The TV talk show *Dr. Phil* even picked up on the playground brawl with its show on November 10, 2003, where the stay-at-home moms were literally put on one side of the room and the working moms on the other to argue over who mothers best. The tension behind the mommy wars, real or assumed, hurt all of us. Instead of raising each other up, we were smacking each other down.

In *The Truth Behind the Mommy Wars: Who Decides What Makes a Good Mother?*, feminist scholar Miriam Peskowitz dissected the issues that impact parents and the social price she paid personally to leave her tenured position as a professor when her daughter was born. "What they all have in common is that today's mothers and fathers are caught between cultural assumptions of an egalitarian society and a cultural reality that is not exactly egalitarian. The parent problem is not a working-mom problem or a stay-at-home-mom problem...The parent problem is a serious structural problem. It's a remnant of an economy that saw men as central and ideal workers and relegated women to supporting roles at home," she writes.[6]

In the past dozen years since that *Times* article ran and the mommy wars and the opt-out generation made headlines, the economy convulsed and certain industries like auto and finance nearly collapsed. Newspapers and magazines folded. Retail and real estate were hit hard. The recession between 2007 and 2009 rocked millions of lives, leaving many families financially vulnerable. In fact, the entire economy has been disrupted since the women who Belkin first wrote about left the workforce. Industries and jobs have contracted, changed, or even disappeared because of technology. During this time, the obsessive, child-centered culture of motherhood has altered too. The "surrendering to motherhood" memoirs of the early 2000s have been replaced with the popular "sh*tty mom" books of today.

In a postrecession world, perhaps moms have cut each other some slack. Today, maybe we are less self-righteous and more prudent. Or maybe the pervasiveness of the hang-it-all-out-there mommy stories that embrace our warts and flaws has put us in a post-mommy-judgment era. Who knows? But if we aren't "at war" and instead show solidarity of the sisterhood, there's no doubt we will have more power to create much-needed change.

OPTING BACK IN

In 2013, ten years after Belkin's "Opt-Out Revolution," Judith Warner revisited those women who left their careers in 2003 in her own *New York Times* piece, "The Opt-Out Generation Wants Back In." What Warner found was that some of the women who a decade earlier felt empowered to drop out were now struggling financially and regretting their choices. One gave up her $500,000 job at Oracle to stay home in her big house to care for her three kids. She is now divorced, living in a rental apartment across from a supermarket, and making 20 percent of her former salary.[7]

The married women who left the workforce in the early 2000s didn't know that the economy would collapse—nobody did. And they also may not have prepared for the financial reality of a divorce, or the death of a spouse, or the existential loss of identity that can come with financial dependence. Back then, many of those women had the breezy, cavalier notion that their prestigious degrees were their insurance policies and they could bounce back in whenever they were ready. Sadly, that was not the case and, for most women, not the reality. Nearly one-third of college-educated women have taken time off to care for their children or for aging family members.

Sylvia Ann Hewlett, founder of the Center for Talent Innovation, has examined just how difficult it is for women to reenter the workforce. According to Hewlett's study published by the *Harvard Business Review*, 37 percent of highly qualified women leave their jobs for extended periods, and of those women only 40 percent find full-time jobs again.[8] She also found that women took a big pay cut when they returned, earning on average 16 percent less than they had before they left the workforce. "It was distressingly difficult to get back on track," Hewlett told Judith Warner in her *Times* piece. And time off also widely differs. A 2015 Harvard Business School report, "Life and Leadership after HBS," surveyed its business school alumnae and found that the length of time the women take themselves out of the workforce after having children varies considerably. Thirty percent of Gen

X and Baby Boomer alumnae caring for children full-time have been out of the workforce for under five years; 22 percent for five to nine years; and 48 percent for ten or more years.[9]

HOW MILLENNIALS FORCE CHANGE

For all of these grim numbers, the good news is that things today are changing. There are encouraging signs of workplaces motivated to bring the women who left back on board. After years of losing female talent, companies are finally realizing what that loss of brain trust and gender balance ultimately means for their businesses. When women leave mid-career, it begins to boomerang into a lack of gender diversity in leadership roles, especially at the top. Numerous studies show that businesses do better with more women in senior positions, so actively recruiting and retaining women is not just the culturally correct thing to do—it's an economic imperative as well.

In the past few years, there has been a push from the law, finance, consulting, and technology industries to fold women back into the workforce. Companies including J.P. Morgan, Goldman Sachs, Credit Suisse, Morgan Stanley, Deloitte, McKinsey, and several major law firms have launched midlife internship and reentry programs. These range from ten-week programs to year-long paid internships to ease women back in to work, refreshing their skills and providing new training where needed.

Millennials, officially the largest segment of the workforce, are also helping to shift the conversation about how to make work, well, work for everyone. They are reimagining the entire structure of the workplace, from the number of hours in each workday to where they actually get stuff done. They are demanding a workplace culture that is more flexible and conducive to having a life outside of their job. Studies have found that Millennials say that they would take a pay cut, forgo a promotion, or be willing to move to better manage work-life demands. According to Pew Research Center, "If they were able to make their current job more flexible, 64 percent of Millennials want to occasionally work from home and 66 percent would like to shift their hours."[10]

The bottom line is that Millennials feel entitled to have a life along with a career and believe technology can enable them to work anywhere at any time. So companies that have grown anxious about losing their female talent together with the job hopping of the Millennials are starting to pay attention. All of this may be the perfect moment for women to get back into the game without the stigma of having taken a hiatus or without feeling marginalized by a flexible work status. This way, so that they can embrace what they've been seeking—a fulfilling career and a family.

Equally promising is the fact that several new companies, led by women and powered by tech platforms that connect, teach, and inspire, are trying to make all of this possible.

HELPING BRING WOMEN BACK TO WORK

About two years after taking a break in her career as deputy general counsel for Major League Baseball (MLB), Jennifer Gefsky was eager to get back to work. Like many ambitious women, Jennifer assumed she would integrate her career into her home life. "I never thought I would leave the workforce, but life happens," Jennifer says. For her, life meant getting pregnant with a third child at forty years old.

For seven years, Jennifer was the most senior female on the management side of MLB. Baseball was part of her bloodline. Jennifer's grandfather was an all-star catcher for the Philadelphia Athletics and played for the New York Yankees, but that's not what motivated her to become one of the top women in sports labor law by the time she was thirty years old. Jennifer had dreamed of becoming an orthopedic surgeon, but medical school cost more than law school, and she was paying her own bills. Jennifer had always worked since she was eleven years old, ironing neighbors' shirts, babysitting, and getting her first W-2 at fourteen years old when she worked at McDonalds.

To pay her way through college, Jennifer worked as a cocktail waitress, a hospital emergency room clerk, and a valet parking attendant. After graduating from the University of Pittsburgh School of Law, Jennifer got a job at the prestigious law firm Proskauer Rose in its sports practice in New York City. She quickly made her mark defending the National Basketball Association. From Proskauer Rose, Jennifer was recruited by MLB into a position she loved and in which she thrived. But with a two-and-a-half-hour commute each day, a crushing travel schedule, and a growing family, she was drowning. Jennifer's husband David was also starting a new real estate development business and was never home. They made the joint decision that Jennifer would take a pause in her career. That pause unexpectedly lasted eight years.

When Jennifer's youngest child Blake started preschool, she began itching all over again, determined to go back to work, but was shocked that she just didn't know how to get back in. After all, getting jobs had never been hard for Jennifer. At thirty years old, she was profiled in *Crain's New York Business* magazine as a "40 Under 40 Rising Star," but now at forty-five, Jennifer felt lost. "I didn't know where to begin, and I realized there were tons of women exactly like me."

In 2016, with her cofounder Niccole Kroll, Jennifer launched the digital recruiting platform Après. Après connects women (mostly Gen Xers) who took time out raising kids with companies seeking talent and diversity. The platform does more than list jobs: It helps to empower women and position them in the workplace. It offers access to career coaches, interviewing tips, and resume writing experts who will rewrite a resume and bio for a fee. The site also helps women message and explain the gaps on their resume and shows how to package volunteer work into transferable skills that have value in the workplace.

Once a fierce legal counsel for sports management, Jennifer is now a champion for Gen X women returning to work. Part advocate, part evangelist, Jennifer meets with companies to persuade HR executives and senior leaders as to the strong value proposition this group of female talent has to offer. She argues that these women, unlike Millennials, won't be looking to opt out—their kids are older now, and they have the skills, gravitas, and motivation to be strong leaders and team players in an organization. It's low risk and high return.

"It's insane to me that companies don't give women like me a longer look, because there is such value," Jennifer says. "We educate companies about not only the value in the employee that you're getting in terms of skills and life experience, but you're also getting reenergized women who are excited to empower others, who won't be opting out again, and who bring loyalty." And at a time when culture is everything, Jennifer believes that bringing these women back on board is adding value in other critical ways. "You're sending a message to your younger workforce and a message to your customers and clients that you believe in gender diversity and that you believe in women and in family values— that's what Millennials are demanding of companies today, a strong culture," Jennifer says.

Finding Value in the Gap Years

One of Après's standard lines is "Don't run from the gap." Jennifer says that the gap in a woman's resume is common and is not going away. Millennials are taking time out too, and the gap period will become just another part of the rhythm of the workplace. Jennifer recommends that women be open and honest and say, "Here's what I've done while I've been out of the paid workforce." Companies don't want to hear that you've baked cookies for your school bake sale, but they do want to hear about your organizational and people skills and how what you've been doing is translatable to the position you're looking to be hired for. "Packaging the volunteer work in a way that transfers back into the workplace is extremely valuable. Women have to understand that there is value there," Jennifer says.

Jennifer is also trying to dispel the myth she often hears that these women don't have the drive or staying power to be strong hires. She says that there is a gross misperception that the women are bored and looking for something to do. Still, Jennifer says most of these women have come back to work out of necessity. Whether it's because they are now divorced or their family circumstances have changed, women need jobs. And given that the span of a career can run forty to fifty years, taking three, five, or even ten years off shouldn't permanently hold women back. "These women are either financially motivated or personally motivated to come back, which are both great for employers," Jennifer says. "They also have something to prove: both their ability and the idea that 'you've taken a chance on me, and I'm going to prove you right.' All of this is very compelling and makes them strong employees."

FROM THE MONKEY BARS TO THE CORNER OFFICE

It's been nearly impossible to book lunch with Jessica Spira, forty-five, whose jammed work schedule as a business development executive at a digital publishing company is packed with meetings and too many conference calls to count. I first met Jessica when our sons were just weeks old as we headed to a "new mommy lunch" on the Upper West Side in New York City, where a sorority of postpartum moms got together each Wednesday to bond over sore nipples, Kegel exercises, and the newness of motherhood. Jessica was my first real "mommy friend." Her baby Zachary slept soundly, while my colicky son shrieked from his stroller.

Jessica was also one of my first interviews for *How She Really Does It.* When I interviewed Jessica for my book, our boys were just about eighteen months old. I interviewed famous and regular professional women, but I also spoke to moms like Jessica who had left their careers to stay home with their kids full-time. For six-and-a-half years, until her daughter Elizabeth started preschool, Jessica was home. "I was very much in the moment those first couple of years until I started making the decision to go back, and then I was projecting ahead," Jessica says.

Jessica says that as her kids got a little older, she became very thoughtful and deliberate about how she would transition back into work. She knew that applying her skills in a volunteer capacity could also translate on a resume. So for nearly three years, Jessica got involved in raising money for Hippo Park, a playground on the Upper West Side of Manhattan. She served on the board for the park's annual fair. She sought strategic partners and sold sponsorships. Revenue grew and the park's programming expanded. "This wasn't about the check you could write, it was about the energy you brought," Jessica says. "It was a diverse group of women, and I had a great time doing it."

Her experience with Hippo Park inspired Jessica to take some classes at New York University on fundraising. Jessica says that she worried that she wouldn't easily land a job again in the private sector because the economy was shaky and the news for women trying to reenter the workforce was depressing. "I didn't think there were any doors open to me," Jessica says. "In the press there was a lot of talk of women dropping out. I assumed I'd have to go into nonprofit. I thought maybe it was a more flexible lifestyle, but then I learned that you work longer hours and they actually pay you less, so that was no longer an option."

While Jessica was growing weary of the full-time at-home routine and thinking of how to get back in, she was also paying attention to the bleak economic forecasts. "During the summer of 2007, the economy was showing some cracks, and I thought, I have ceded all of my financial independence to my spouse, but he's in the financial industry and that's really not dependable anymore, so I better get my shit together and figure something out," Jessica says. "I had been on LinkedIn and had a decent network and always kept up with people, so I was able to re-light that really quickly."

Jessica tapped into her network. She had people who she trusted look over her resume and offer feedback. She listed and detailed her volunteer work and explained the big gap in her professional life. Within weeks of first connecting with former colleagues on LinkedIn, Jessica was interviewing. "When people asked me what I was most proud of professionally, I would say the Hippo Park work. I really pounded the pavement," Jessica says. "It was business development, just in a different way than I had done before. But I went on interviews and parlayed that experience into my conversations." Within six weeks of first interviewing, Jessica had found a full-time job. She says that women need to realize that time doesn't stand still when you take time out. Your new boss could be younger than you and your title could be frozen, if not downgraded. "You have to check your ego and be prepared to eat a little bit of crow," Jessica says. "I went back to the level I left at. You have to be okay reporting to someone your age or younger. And your comp and title can take a big hit too. You have to get comfortable with that."

Coming Back Stronger

Jessica was thrilled to have found a full-time position just as the economy started tanking. She was cognizant about working hard. Even though her company gave Summer Fridays, she rarely took them. She knew there were times when she would need to leave early for soccer games, doctor appointments, or other kid stuff, so she intentionally worked later when she could. "I just thought, from an optics perspective, I wanted them to see that I was all in," Jessica says. "I never wanted to be the person where they say, 'Yeah, she's the mom' and 'Oh, she's not here or she's always late.'

Jessica has been back to work for six years now. She's had three jobs and several promotions and has recently reached the level she believes she would have been at if she hadn't taken time off. She doesn't apologize for staying home with her kids or regret what for her was a true choice. And like many moms in the workplace, she sees an added benefit to motherhood.

"Frankly, I'm a much better employee now that I am a mom, and I am better able to manage people," Jessica says. "I have a different way of approaching things than a lot of my younger colleagues. It sounds like a cliché, but I am older, wiser, and more confident, and I don't get rattled by the small stuff. I'm also a lot more fearless than I was before."

This is exactly the message Jennifer Gefsky wants companies to hear and what Après is preaching. The mom who takes time off comes back as a stronger employee and a better manager. The Gen Xer is going to over-perform to show her value and loyalty. She also brings a level of experience and maturity to counterbalance the younger, less experienced Millennial workforce.

And for Après, the timing may be perfect.

"No one bats an eye when I say I took a six-year leave. It's more accepted now," Jessica says. "But my advice is that your network is the most important thing you have. Whatever you do, leave on good terms and stay close to the people who you work for, because you don't know when you're going to need them. Also, try to keep up your skills if you can or be able to position your skills in a way that's relevant. It's incredibly important."

THE WORST QUESTION. EVER.

"So, what do you do? I hate that question," Lisa Skeete Tatum, forty-seven, tells me as we sit in a Corner Bakery booth in a mall on the outskirts of Princeton, New Jersey. She's not alone. I hate that question too. Sometimes, it's been easy to answer. I'm a TV producer! I'm a Capitol Hill press secretary! I'm an author! I'm an editor-in-chief of a website! Hooray! And then other times, when I was working in public relations but not wanting to call myself only a publicist (because well, I've always had a complicated relationship with that job description), I would want to say, "I work in PR but I'm also an author *and* a producer." But that sounded lame, like I was apologizing for PR, making excuses for my current gig. And I felt like a loser to be living in the past. But much worse is when I'm not gainfully employed and have no legitimate title or paycheck and call myself a freelancer or consultant. That feels like a euphemism for: "I can't find a job. No one will hire me."

It doesn't feel liberating; it feels small.

For many women who are underemployed or unemployed or employed in areas they don't want to be, the "What do you do?" question strikes at something deeply personal, a hidden reservoir of messy emotion teeming with anxiety. Typically an innocuous question (though at times cloaked in judgment), it can be a painful reminder of some unfinished business in a woman's career ambition. It can unleash feelings of inadequacy, insecurity, and existential angst.

"It stirs an inner conflict," says Nikki Kessler, forty-four, a sea-soned Los Angeles entertainment producer, who co-owns 99 Arms Productions, a full-service independent production com-pany. A feast-or-famine industry to begin with, Hollywood's dig-ital disruption has forced many entertainment veterans to scramble and figure out their next move. "I hadn't intentionally retired, but we weren't getting work," Nikki says. "My kids were little, and I started to accept the fact that maybe this was my 'mommy time,' and I tried to disassociate myself from my work identity. But I struggled with that because I spent a big portion of my life creating that identity for myself, and that is hard to release."

After nearly three years of not having a project in prodjection, Nikki and her business partner Jennifer Gore were recently asked to produce a scripted comedy series for Warner Bros' digital di-vision and LeBron James's production company, SpringHill En-tertainment. Despite a tight budget, terrible pay, and even worse hours, it was an opportunity they couldn't refuse. "We did it be-cause digital is the future, despite the fact that there's no money in it," Nikki says. "Ultimately, it felt like [we should] jump in and get on board and then afterwards reassess if we want to do it again, because this is where entertainment is moving. Either we need to embrace it or it will pass us by, and we go the way of the dinosaurs."

Karen Shnek Lippman, a managing partner at executive search firm Koller Search Partners, would agree with Nikki's in-stinct to seize the opportunity—even if it's not initially lucrative or ideal. As industries like media, marketing, and entertainment change rapidly, you may have to play the long game if you hope to get back in. "Once you dip your toe into the water and say you can beat this, you can be very successful," Shnek Lippman says. "But it requires opening up your mind and teaching yourself to accept that you have to forget about the past somewhat and just go guns blazing into the future of whatever industry you're in. You will have to figure out how to get the skills and experience you need in order to thrive again."

GETTING UNSTUCK

More than forty million professional women will find themselves at a crossroads in their career, says Lisa Skeete Tatum, the CEO and cofounder of Landit, a digital platform that launched in 2016, aiming to be an amped up LinkedIn for women. They will hit these "inflection points,"—as Lisa calls them—moments of change—because of a whole host of issues that are personally and professionally driven. Landit bills itself as an entirely new approach for women who are stuck, looking to make their next move, or simply wanting to achieve more. The question every woman faces, the website says, is "Where do I start?"

Like Jennifer Gefsky's Après platform, the Landit business was birthed from a personal place. Lisa felt stuck. She may be the last woman who you would imagine would feel that way. After all, Lisa defied all types of odds, bushwhacking her own unconventional path from Newark to Cambridge. Born to a single mom in Newark, New Jersey, Lisa and her mom left Newark when she was five years old, after race riots engulfed the city. They hopscotched between Europe and the States because of her mom's job as a military nurse. Lisa landed at Princeton University, where she majored in chemical engineering—as an African American woman in engineering, she was a minority among a minority at Princeton. After graduating, she worked for Procter and Gamble and then joined a start-up, which led to Harvard Business School.

For eleven years, Lisa worked in early stage health care venture capital in a three-person firm in Princeton, New Jersey. She sat on prestigious boards and had an enviable pedigree, and yet this mother of two boys felt unsure of what to do. Despite all of her connections and experience, she wasn't clear what she was looking for or even how she should ask her contacts to help her. Simply, she didn't know her next move. "As we progress, figuring out that next pivot is challenging, and you may have the clarity on what doesn't fit, but you may not know what it is that does fit," Lisa says. "When you are young, you have the whole world in front of you. But when you have a little bit of history and a track record, the world looks a little different."

Lisa was preaching to the choir. It's exactly what I've experienced and frankly what inspired this book. Even with strong networks and job experience, you may not know what path to take and who could help lead you there.

In 2012, Lisa was nominated for the Henry Crown Fellowship Program through The Aspen Institute. The goal of the program is for fellows to create positive change in the world. They need to leave with a big, ambitious project. "As I was going through this personal transition, I realized my project was me," Lisa says. "I realized how many millions of women were in similar positions and in many ways suffering in silence because you don't want people to know that you don't have it figured out or you don't know what's next, and you're feeling vulnerable."

Lisa is not afraid to show that vulnerability—in fact, it's what she thinks makes Landit so powerful. The issues wrapped up in women's career pivots, reentries, or total relaunches are complicated and often loaded with feelings of insecurity, fear, and anxiety. All of this can lead to depression or inertia or both. Landit wants to help resolve this cocktail of conflict.

"I can't tell you how many times I've gone around the room and people say, 'Life is great.' But then someone starts talking and the confessions come pouring out," Lisa says.

On Landit, women input information about their goals, paid work, and volunteer experience, as well as their work schedule preferences and skills so they can receive personalized job listings, a career "playbook," and access to services from resume writing and interviewing to brand-building. Landit gives value and legitimacy to the PTA and soccer mom experience. Aside from helping women build confidence, Landit, like Après, shows women how their volunteer work can translate. Just as Jessica Spira successfully wove her work with Hippo Park into her resume, Landit models how to effectively explain the non-paid piece of what many women have pursued.

Will You Be My Mentor?

For years now, mentors and sponsors have become popular concepts in the workplace. A sponsor is someone in a senior position who is willing to make a bet on your behalf, spend the time to get to know you, and would use some political capital to pull you up through the ranks. A mentor, on the other hand, can give feedback on how to grow your career. She can offer advice and wisdom about your industry, help you network, and teach you new skills. Ideally, it would be awesome to have a squad of people to help raise and support you as you grow and actively advocate for you. And that's exactly what Lisa wants Landit to help cultivate. The platform walks you through creating a personal "board of advisors," which it sees as critical. Lisa is trying to reimagine the mentor and sponsor relationship. "I have never seen a wildly successful mentorship program, because it's too heavy—that whole 'Will you be my mentor?' approach. You can't force it. Instead, you need to create a relationship, and then say, 'I am coming to you because I need this,'" Lisa says.

Women are also unsure how to engage with their mentors or sponsors. It can be an awkward relationship. So Landit wants to help women frame the conversation and the "ask" before they set up a meeting. Early in Lisa's career, her boss told her that she would arrange a conversation with a more senior person at the company, and her advice was "don't waste that bullet." That's stuck with Lisa ever since. Be armed and ready for the moment. People generally want to help but are busy and can't be bothered to think too hard about what they could do for you. Specific, directed requests are much more effective. "You have to come prepared. And yes, you form a personal relationship because it can't be all transactional, but if you're going to take somebody's time you better come with an ask or with a question," Lisa says.

Sell Yourself

As we discussed in chapter 9, branding today is important for everyone, but arguably more so for those who have had untraditional career paths or interruptions. Landit seeks to help women craft their narrative. It walks women through what Lisa calls a "Mad Libs" fill-in-the-sentence approach to building a brand statement, distilling it into meaningful messages. "We notoriously undersell ourselves. But if you don't tell your story well, and you don't frame your successes and interruptions, and you don't present your accomplishments to an employer, you can look risky and you won't get a shot. When the conversations are happening, your name isn't in them," Lisa says. "I also think when you have a brand identity, it helps inform some of the choices that you make. There's a plan and you're being intentional."

After opting out or getting pushed off the career track, many women want to get back in. Taking the shame out of not having a job or feeling unfocused is something Lisa takes to heart. For her, Landit is personal. "I feel like everything I've done in my life has led me to this," Lisa says. "If you're isolated and you don't have a way to talk about it, and you think that there are no options, and you feel like you have no skills, even though you used to do all of these amazing things, it's terrible. I'm doing this because I feel so deeply and I'm so passionate about it, and because I can. If not me, who?"

A DIFFERENT MODEL FOR
GETTING BACK IN

By 2020, it's anticipated that more than 40 percent of the workforce will be freelancers, contractors, and temporary employees. The phenomenon of the "free agent" professional was discussed in a 2012 *Harvard Business Review* article, "The Rise of the Supertemp." In it, Jodi Greenstone Miller and Matt Miller wrote about how the best and the brightest were leaving the full-time workforce and upending the economy.[11] Valuing autonomy and flexibility over the endless grind of meetings and long commutes, they were choosing a different path—a project-based one. They could work when they wanted and how they wanted and still earn high-paying incomes. Sound elitist and unrealistic? Perhaps. But the trend in talent-based, project-based matching is on the rise, and for obvious reasons it may be most welcomed by moms who feel shoved out of their careers and want back in on their own terms.

It is this model that former college roommates Kate Motley, forty-one, and Laxmi Wordham, forty, are creating with Athenity, an online marketplace they launched in June 2015 that connects professional women with project-based work. They've discovered that the sweet spot for finding temporary work across industries is from smaller groups within large companies or smaller midsize companies. However, they make it clear that Athenity is not just for moms, but for all women seeking a more accommodating work-life situation.

Like Après and Landit, and perhaps all businesses guided by a true mission, Athenity's origin story emerges from its founders' own struggles. Kate's last job was leading marketing and product development for a toy company. Laxmi worked as the chief digital officer at the Michael J. Fox Foundation. Moves from New York City to the suburbs—Kate to Connecticut and Laxmi to Westchester, New York—meant long commutes, little time with their kids, and, ultimately, them both leaving their jobs. The urgency of finding an alternative solution for themselves and for their female friends who also felt pushed out of the workforce inspired Athenity.

"We've been struck by how many women would be working and could be working but aren't; and the longer they are out, the more intimidating it is to step back in," Laxmi says. "Where we come in is pounding the pavement to find the work and to get companies to say, yes, this is a model that we believe in. The gig economy is growing and a whole switch is underway, but a lot of companies haven't fully embraced that yet."

Like Jennifer Gefsky and Lisa Skeete Tatum, Laxmi and Kate are evangelists for folding women back into the workforce and rethinking how to retain female talent, especially after they become mothers. "We really are mission driven and that's what gets us up in the morning, that's what we really care about, that's what excites us," Kate says. "We want to advocate and change the model and get more companies to buy into this sea change. Providing an alternative model for women is important for all of us."

12

WHAT'S YOUR STORY?

THERE IS AN ADAGE THAT you write what you know. For many writers, another truth is that you write about what you *need* to know. This book is both for me. The heart of *Fearless and Free* had marinated in my head for years as I pivoted from one job to the next, often struggling with how to shape my story, showcase my varied skills, and shoehorn into the positions that I wanted. For the eighteen months that I researched and wrote this book, I tried on many of the celebrated ideas and concepts steeped in Silicon Valley culture. Some, like failure, I already knew well.

When I was working at *Dateline NBC*, my college roommate Barbara Messing and I had an idea for what we imagined would be a perfect made-for-MTV backpacking travel series, cheekily called "The Gringo Trail." We took vacation time, secured a bank loan, hired a cameraman and host, flew to Ecuador, and taped for a week. Sadly, MTV would never see the pilot. The tapes we shot literally went up in flames at 30 Rock when a freak electrical fire incinerated my NBC office—and *only* my office.

Years later, I spent nearly a year developing and shooting a documentary about sleepaway camp only to lose the funding and, consequently, my interest. I ran for School Board in my New Jersey town and got beaten in a landslide. And I poured my heart into a charming children's book about girl power, but was rejected by every publisher and told that I needed to turn my ten-year-old female protagonist into a farm animal. So I have a close relationship with failure, but perhaps an even stronger one with the growth that comes from the uncomfortable and often depressing experience. In fact, I probably wouldn't be writing *Fearless and Free* if I hadn't failed many times before.

Through the extraordinary process of creating this book, I became much more aware of the need to be intentional about engineering my own serendipity. I started actively seeking opportunities where I put myself in the same space with the people I needed to know. I sought out female networks like Rachel Sklar and Glynnis MacNicol's TheLi.st. Instead of being a silent member of the group, I fought my natural instinct and actively engaged, going to as many events as I could. And the more I connected, the more authentic the experience became. The urgency to network and to network well became more apparent with everyone I interviewed. I'll be clear: I am not a natural networker. I'm out there, but I'm faking it. I'm pushing myself to be present, forcing myself to show up and to work the room. For years, I sort of fell off the professional radar, consumed by caring for my kids and going to jobs that I didn't necessarily love but that helped pay the bills. I felt crunched. Networking seemed like something to do when I had extra time, which I felt I never had. But more importantly, I didn't enjoy it. I dreaded it.

Industry events can be boring and lonely and expensive—they're hard to justify if you are paying the fee and induce anxiety that you're not maximizing the experience and meeting the people you should be meeting. There's a gnawing feeling that you're missing out. I wandered around the streets of Austin at SXSW in a sea of forty thousand people for four days, largely alone. So when I met Shelley Zalis and her Girls' Lounge, where the brilliant premise is to create a women's space at conferences so you don't feel alone but empowered, it hit home with me.

The day before the manuscript for this book was due, I traveled to Washington, DC, for the first-ever White House State of Women Summit. My book was not yet finished. I had nearly one hundred footnotes to add, editing to do, and this last chapter to write. I had no hotel reservation—they were virtually sold out—and no one specifically to spend the day-long conference with. I had only a hazy sense of what I would actually get out of the conference. Yes, First Lady Michelle Obama and Oprah would be there—for most women that was reason enough to go. And yet still, I agonized. Do I spend the money for an Amtrak ticket? Is it crazy to travel the day before my book is due? Is it really worth it? I did know that many women from TheLi.st network would be there, and the women behind the Girls' Lounge and the Landit platform were also going. I bought my train ticket. I really did want to hear Oprah interview the First Lady, but more important, I *needed* to network. I *needed* to be in that room.

I showed up a few hours late, but the squad from TheLi.st had secured tables for all of us. I was getting updates from a WhatsApp group chat. It was clear I wouldn't be alone. Almost immediately, Susan McPherson, a corporate social responsibility and communications superstar who I knew only from her listserv posts that brimmed with encouraging words to women, offered to host a book party for me. Others were equally enthusiastic and supportive. I was fully realizing the power of an engaged network and how professionally and emotionally important it was in that moment.

As I stood in line for a free hummus snack, one of the few men at the conference asked me that dreaded question, "So what do you do?" "I'm just a writer," I answered. "I'm a writer too," he said sweetly. "You need to take the 'just' out." For whatever reason, my "just" slipped in. But he was right. And I realized the irony of the moment—I'm at a White House State of Women Summit, hours before my book manuscript was due, and I had called myself "just a writer." I had diminished my own power with a single word, and crazily enough, was a progressive dude who called me out on it.

And then of course, I thought of Tami Reiss and her "Just Not Sorry" Gmail plug-in and how her life's story weirdly embodies almost every theme of this book.

A THREAD RUNS THROUGH IT

It was winter quarter of freshman year at UCLA when Tami Reiss spent the night in the hospital with her friend Mary, who was dehydrated and achy from the flu. Fiercely chatty, Tami peppered the doctors and nurses with so many incisive questions about Mary's condition that everyone asked her if she was pre-med. She wasn't. She was in civil engineering. But a few days after Mary was released, Tami switched majors. Medical school wouldn't be for her—she couldn't imagine the grind of MCAT prep, let alone at least eight more tedious years of school—but physiology, the science of the body systems and how they perform and dance with each other, intrigued Tami. It was nature's brilliantly designed human operating system.

At UCLA, Tami interned as an athletic trainer on a campus known for churning out Olympic champions and logged more than five hundred hours in physical therapy observation. She loved the creative expression of physical therapy—more art than science and very hands-on. Wanting to help others was as much a part of Tami's DNA as her curly brown hair. She was back home in North Miami Beach for Thanksgiving senior year when a friend mentioned that she was going to the University of Florida after graduation to get an MBA. Tami thought that sounded like a smart idea for her too—after all, if she planned to run her own physical therapy business someday, she should know at least something about accounting. During the ten-month master's program, Tami took a social entrepreneur class that made her realize that she didn't miss physical therapy. Instead, she wanted to work in the nonprofit space. She thrived on touching and helping people—in whatever form that took.

After graduating, Tami packed up and moved back to Los Angeles, where she found a job on Craigslist that still remains one of the most formative in her career—working for the Muscular Dystrophy Association. Tami fundraised, ran events, and organized legions of volunteers. Tami thought her next obvious move would be into consulting, but she was rejected from every consulting firm, including the nonprofits. Tami kept hearing that she lacked the rigorous finance and math background required. College calculus was a bust; it's partly why she happily switched from civil engineering into physiology. But now Tami needed to fill in her gaps.

Determined to learn some "big math" and become familiar with wonky organizational processes, Tami got a job with Farmers Insurance Group. Farmers was a legacy business, a snooze compared to modern-day start-ups. But Tami realized she needed experience in areas where she was lacking and being on the product marketing team, even at Farmers, would expose her to new possibilities. Predictably, things at an old-school insurance company move at a glacier pace, so after about a year and a half at Farmers, Tami was itching to jump into the burgeoning and electric tech scene of Los Angeles in 2009.

Tami scored an internship at Tsavo Media with Mike Jones, a hot-shot founder and multi-millionaire entrepreneur who ruled the cult world of Santa Monica start-ups and would go on to become the CEO of Myspace. Working out of an art deco building overlooking the ocean in downtown Santa Monica, Tami was among her tribe of creative doers. With $10,000 of her own money and another $10,000 borrowed from her parents, while still interning Tami launched an iPhone app called Star Trax, a celebrity news aggregator. "With Star Trax, I was now a cool tech entrepreneur, but I did everything I possibly could have done wrong," Tami says. Fast-talking and irrepressibly enthusiastic, Tami was a natural networker. The process of building her app deepened her connections to the L.A. tech community and gave her some valuable street cred as she pondered her next move.

As if by divine intervention, that move came in a phone call from Rachel, a friend from Tami's synagogue. Tami had recently volunteered to run a synagogue fundraising dinner at Rachel's sister's house. It was a big success. Tech company Cornerstone OnDemand was looking to fill a project manager position. They had interviewed scores of engineers with hardcore techie backgrounds but couldn't find anyone they liked. Cornerstone's CEO Adam Miller knew Tami because he had served as synagogue president a few years earlier when Tami had set up a management tool to connect temple members online. Rachel and Adam didn't know details about Tami's professional background, but they felt if she could masterfully organize those temple activities, then she could project manage for their clients.

Tami at first thought this was absurd. It was a leap. She had been a fundraiser and party planner for the Muscular Dystrophy Association, had worked on a product team at Farmers Insurance but hadn't produced anything, and for almost two years had worked as an intern at two start-ups. But then Tami started to reframe her experience, thinking about what she had done and what she knew how to do well. At the Muscular Dystrophy Association, she not only organized volunteers, but also had to *motivate* volunteers—what she had done *was* project management. She had helped run big events with a finite deadline to deliver. There were targets and goals and budgets to meet. Tech companies also have extreme deadlines and products to deliver. They run on tight budgets and high expectations from investors and shareholders. Tami had never managed engineers or clients before, but she had managed people—and aren't engineers and clients humans too?

Tami got the gig.

An Unlikely CEO

Skip ahead a few years, and Tami was living in New York City. She was still not a coder; in fact, she says she'll never learn how to code and will tell you that not everyone should. But she loves the infectious creative vibe of the start-up space. She thrives on constantly iterating and making things better: making her products better, making herself better. It was 2013 when a friend, an investor, called to say he was looking for a CEO for his company that created coding efficiencies for companies. Tami suggested a few names. But he said he has a better idea: Why didn't Tami become the CEO? She thought this was ridiculous. She was thirty-two years old and had never run a company, let alone even managed a large team. And, most glaringly, she didn't code.

But when the investor described what he needed, Tami saw how her experience *could* make sense. Maybe it wasn't such a stretch. The work—at least, a part of it (the marketing and project-management piece)—was in her wheelhouse. Tami accepted the job, but with a surprising caveat. "I took on a chief product officer title. I was afraid of the CEO title because I didn't think I deserved it," Tami says. "If you want to talk about the impostor syndrome, try jumping seven levels from individual contributor to CEO, from never having managed a team to managing a company."

The list of accomplished people plagued by the impostor syndrome is an impressive one. Tina Fey, Maya Angelou, Sheryl Sandberg, and Lena Dunham have each publicly confessed to experiencing that angsty feeling of phoniness—that feeling that you don't belong and you're not worthy of the recognition or position, despite your talent. You feel like a fraud and fear being found out.[1]

It was not lost on Tami that a guy would never turn down a CEO title. But Tami needed to prove herself, not to the investor who believed in her but to *herself.* A few months later, Tami leaned into her strengths and launched a Female Founders event for New York City's women in tech. It was a wild success, and after that Tami readily claimed her position as the CEO of Cyrus Innovation.

About a year later in 2015, Tami was suddenly catapulted to fame as the email etiquette guru when her Gmail plug-in "Just Not Sorry" hit the scene. Yes, this is the same Tami from chapter 1 who had an idea at a brunch with girlfriends that she should do something about the sorry state of women's communication. And that idea turned into an email empowerment tool. Tami is now invited to speak at Google, Citi, Goldman Sachs, and women's conferences around the country about female email communication, which has added yet another dimension to her unusual career path—one that for her makes perfect sense. "There is a thread through all of it," Tami says, smiling.

But Tami will be the first to remind you that not everything always works out for her. She spent four years at one job where she was never going to move ahead. She watched colleagues *she* had hired get promoted and rise above her. Tami has also been rejected from positions because she didn't have the experience a hiring manager was looking for, no matter how expertly she spun her varied background. And not every project she launches takes off brilliantly. In fact, some have flopped fabulously.

Connecting the Dots

Still, Tami's story reflects so many of the concepts that drive the success of Silicon Valley. She takes risks, which has strengthened her confidence. She has a growth mindset and grows from failure. She iterates, engineers her serendipity, and actively networks. She leverages her work experience—both paid and volunteer—and applies it in new directions to maximize that "adjacent possible," the place that hovers on the edge of future possibilities. And ultimately, Tami is her own best publicist, perhaps especially because her path is unique, and she must connect the dots for people. "When people look at what I've done, they are confused. I have to explain it more than other people it seems," Tami says. "And I'm sure the investors who hired me have second-guessed themselves over the years. We've done good things that worked and others that didn't, and I iterated. That's what product managers are supposed to do. You put something out into the world, and you monitor it, and you say okay, that's not successful so let's pivot. Or if it is working, let's keep going."

And that is a smart lesson for all of us women.

Notes

INTRODUCTION

1 Katty Kay and Claire Shipman, *The Confidence Code: The Science and Art of Self-Assurance—What Women Should Know* (New York: Harper Collins, 2014), xvi.

2 Ibid., 21.

3 "After the Backlash Barbie Gets a New Set of Skills," *All Things Considered* (NPR). Podcast audio, Nov. 22, 2014, http://www.npr.org/2014/11/22/365968465/after-backlash-computer-engineer-barbie-gets-new-set-of-skills/.

4 Glynnis MacNicol, "Flip Flopping Is Now Essential to Getting Ahead," *ELLE*, May 20, 2015.

5 Reid Hoffman and Ben Casnocha, *The Start-Up of You: Adapt to the Future, Invest in Yourself, and Transform Your Career* (New York: Crown Business, 2012), 8–9.

6 Heather Long, "The New Normal: 4 Changes by the Time You're 32," *CNN Money*, April 12, 2016, http://money.cnn.com/2016/04/12/news/economy/millennials-change-jobs-frequently/.

CHAPTER 1: CHANGE YOUR WORDS: BOOST YOUR BRAND

1 Jessica Bennett, "I'm Sorry, But Women Really Need to Stop Apologizing," *Time*, June 18, 2014; Melissa Dahl, "Sorry I'm Not Sorry, I'm Sorry," *New York*, June 20, 2014.

2 Emma Gray, "Amy Schumer's 'I'm Sorry' Skewers a Culture That Makes Women Apologize Constantly," *The Huffington Post*, May, 14, 2015, http://www.huffingtonpost.com/2015/05/14/amy-schumer-im-sorry-not-sorry_n_7276504.html/.

3 Alexandra Petri, "Famous Quotes the Way a Woman Would Have to Say Them During a Meeting," *The Washington Post*, October 13, 2015.

4 "The Double Bind Dilemma for Women in Leadership: Damned If You Do, Doomed If You Don't," Catalyst, July 2007, http://www.catalyst.org/knowledge/double-bind.

5 Deborah Tannen, "Our Impossible Expectations of Hillary Clinton and All Women in Authority," *Washington Post*, February 19, 2016.

6 Colby Itkowitz, "Little Marco, 'Lyin' Ted,' 'Crooked Hillary': How Donald Trump Makes Name Calling Stick," *Washington Post*, April 20, 2016.

7 April Siese, "Seven Memorable Quotes from Hillary Clinton's 1995 Women's Rights Speech That Are Still Meaningful Today," *Bustle*, September 6, 2015.

8 Chris Cillizza, "Hillary Clinton, 18 Million Cracks and the Power of Making History," *Washington Post*, June 13, 2013.

9 "The Photograph That Has Everyone Texting Hillary Clinton," *Time*, April 9, 2012, http://time.com/3787649/texting-hillary-clinton/.

10 Jimmy Kimmel, "Hillary Clinton, Peter Krause, Music from Fifth Harmony," *Jimmy Kimmel Live!*, ABC, March 24, 2016.

11 Robin Lakoff, "Nice and Tough," Robinlakoff.com, Jan. 19, 2016, http://robinlakoff.com/language/nice-and-tough/.

12 Robin Lakoff, "Listening to Her: Reprise," Robinlakoff.com, March 22, 2016, http://robinlakoff.com/language/listening-to-her-reprise/.

13 Ibid.

14 Kieran Snyder, "The Abrasiveness Trap: High Achieving Men and Women Are Described Differently in Reviews," *Fortune*, August 26, 2014.

15 Jennifer Lawrence, "Why Do I Make Less Than My Male Co-Stars?" *Lenny Letter*, October 12, 2015.

16 Tamar Gottesman, "Beyoncé Wants to Change the Conversation," *ELLE*, April 4, 2016.

CHAPTER 2: STRIKE A POSE AND FEEL THE POWER

1 Amy Cuddy, *Presence: Bringing Your Boldest Self to Your Biggest Challenges* (New York: Little, Brown and Company, 2015), 19.

2 Ibid., 24.

3 "Bringing 'Presence to Your Life,'" *Here and Now* (WBUR-FM). Podcast audio, Dec. 22, 2015, http://www.wbur.org/hereandnow/2015/12/22/presence-amy-cuddy.

4 Ibid.

5 Cuddy, *Presence*, chapter 8.

6 Hunter Schwartz, "A Remarkable Photo of President Obama and Angela Merkel," *Washington Post*, June 8, 2015.

7 Kay and Shipman, *The Confidence Code*, xx.

8 Ibid., 61–62.

9 Ibid., 62.

10 Ibid., 21–23.

11 Ibid., 23.

12 Kitty Kay and Claire Shipman, "The Confidence Gap," *The Atlantic*, May 2014.

13 Ibid., 145.

14 Carol Dweck, *Mindset: The New Psychology of Success* (New York: Ballantine Books, 2006).

15 Ibid., 141.

16 Cindi Leive, "Career Advice from Hillary Rodham Clinton: "'You Don't Have to be Perfect, Most Men Never Think Like Tha,'" *Glamour*, August 7, 2014.

17 Sheryl Sandberg, *Lean In: Women, Work and the Will to Lead* (New York: Knopf, 2013), 62.

CHAPTER 3: CREATE YOUR OWN SERENDIPITY

1 Horace Walpole, "The Invention of *Serendipity*," *The Paris Review*, Jan. 28, 2016.

2 Steven Johnson, *Where Good Ideas Come From: The Natural History of Innovation* (New York: Riverhead Books, 2010), 31.

3 Ibid., 41.

4 Malcolm Gladwell, *Outliers: The Story of Success* (New York: Little, Brown and Company, 2008), 155.

5 Ann Friedman, "Shine Theory: Why Powerful Women Make the Greatest Friends," *New York*, May 31, 2013.

6 Adam Grant, *Give and Take: Why Helping Others Drives Our Success* (New York: Penguin, 2013), 55, 58.

CHAPTER 4: NETWORKING IN THE GIRLS' LOUNGE: THE POWER OF CONNECTIONS

1 Brooks Barnes, "Networking in the 'Girls' Lounge,'" *New York Times*, March 5, 2016.

2 Rachel Sklar, "I'm 41, Single and Pregnant," Medium.com, Oct. 29, 2014, https://medium.com/thelist/im-41-single-and-pregnant-9b2da840a45a#.t4yjlbkfm.

3 Malcolm Gladwell, *The Tipping Point: How Little Things Can Make a Big Difference* (New York: Little, Brown and Company, 2000), 55.

4 Ibid., 51.

5 Shane Snow, *Smartcuts: How Hackers, Innovators, and Icons Accelerate Success* (New York: HarperCollins, 2014), 124.

6 Grant, *Give and Take.*

7 Reid Hoffman, "Why Relationships Matter: I-to-the-We," LinkedIn.com, November 6, 2012, https://www.linkedin.com/pulse/20121106193412-1213-why-relationships-matter-i-to-the-we/.

8 Jacob Morgan, "Why Every Employee Should Be Building Weak Ties at Work," *Forbes*, March 11, 2014.

9 Athena Vongalis-Macrow, "Assess the Value of your Networks," *Harvard Business Review*, June 29, 2012.

10 Ibid.

11 Grant, *Give and Take*, 220.

CHAPTER 5: FALLING FROM THE TOP: RISING WITH RESILIENCE

1 Ken Auletta, "Jill Abramson and the Times: What Went Wrong?," *New Yorker*, May 15, 2014.

2 Juliet Eilperin, "White House Women Want to be in the Room Where It Happens," *Washington Post*, Sept. 13, 2016.

3 Mark Berman, "Watch Jill Abramson's Commencement Speech at Wake Forest," *Washington Post*, May 19, 2014.

4 Jill Abramson, "Struck on the Street: Four Survivors," *New York Times*, May 2, 2014.

CHAPTER 6: CONGRATULATIONS, YOU'RE FIRED!

1 Dan Lyons, "Congratulations! You've Been Fired," *New York Times*, April 9, 2016.

2 Ibid.

3 Ibid.

4 Reid Hoffman, Ben Casnocha, and Chris Yeh, *The Alliance: Managing Talent in the Networked Age* (Boston: Harvard Business Review Press, 2014).

5 Patty McCord, "How Netflix Reinvented HR," *Harvard Business Review*, Jan.–Feb. 2014.

6 Deborah Copaken Kogan, "My So-Called 'Post-Feminist Life' in Arts and Letters," *The Nation*, April 9, 2013.

7 Deborah Copaken, "Harvard Grad, 48, Loses Job and Insurance, Gets Rejected by The Container Store," Forbes.com (repost from Cafe.com), Nov. 4, 2014, http://www.forbes.com/sites/nextavenue/2014/11/04/harvard-grad-48-loses-job-and-insurance-gets-rejected-by-container-store/#71a032695331.

8 KJ Dell'Antonia, "Writer, Rejected for a Retail Job, Is Embraced and Vilified on Facebook," *New York Times*, Nov. 3, 2014.

CHAPTER 7: FLIPPING OFF FAILURE

1 "Hillary Clinton Endorses Barack Obama," *New York Times*, Transcript of Hillary Clinton Concession Speech, June 7, 2008.

2 Candice M. Hughes, "How Women Entrepreneurs Can Accelerate to Break Out Growth," Forbes.com, Dec. 1, 2014; Dan Primack, "Women Are Not Making Progress in Male-Dominated VC World, Data Shows," *Fortune*, Jan. 30, 2015.

3 Kevin Roose, "The Failure Fetish in Silicon Valley," *New York*, March 25, 2014.

4 George Bradt, "Want to Fail Fast, Do These Things," *Forbes*, Jan. 23, 2013.

5 Ryan Holiday, "Why You Should Embrace Failure," *Psychology Today*, May 12, 2014.

6 Kay and Shipman, *The Confidence Code*, 140.

7 Dweck, *Mindset*, 6–7; 15.

8 Ibid., 12.

CHAPTER 8: ITERATE. MEDITATE. REPEAT.

1 "Camp Gyno," YouTube video, posted by Helloflo, July 28, 2013.

2 "First Moon Party," YouTube video, posted by Helloflo, August 2014.

3 Russell Simmons, "Russell Simmons: 3 Simple Ways Meditation Will Make You a Better Entrepreneur," *Entrepreneur*, March 8, 2014.

4 "Russell Simmons Explains Finding Success Through Stillness," Rollingout.com, March 7, 2014, http://rollingout.com/2014/03/07/russell-simmons-explains-finding-success-stillness/.

CHAPTER 9: MOTHERS OF REINVENTION

1 Sam Laird, "The Rise of the Mommy Blogger," Mashable.com, May 8, 2012, http://mashable.com/2012/05/08/mommy-blogger-infographic/#yz6ZwVnJmkqG.

2 Lisa Belkin, "Queen of the Mommy Bloggers," *New York Times*, Feb. 23, 2011.

3 Gillian B. White, "Women Are Owning More and More Small Businesses," *The Atlantic*, April 17, 2015.

4 Ibid.

CHAPTER 10: BRANDING IS NOT BRAGGING

1 Aliza Licht, *Leave Your Mark: Land Your Dream Job. Kill It in Your Career. Rock Social Media* (New York: Grand Central Publishing, 2015), 201–202.

2 Kirsten Fleming, "The 'DKNY PR Girl' Reveals How to Get Out of a Career Rut," *New York Post,* May 4, 2015.

3 Meredith Fineman, "What Your Professional Bio Needs to Get Noticed," *Harvard Business Review,* March 2, 2015.

CHAPTER 11: GETTING BACK IN

1 Lisa Belkin, "The Opt-Out Revolution," *New York Times Magazine,* Oct. 26, 2003.

2 Leslie Stahl, "October 10, 2004," *60 Minutes,* CBS, Oct. 2004.

3 Heather Hewett, "Telling It Like It Is: Rewriting the Opt-Out Narrative," Mothersmovement.org, Oct. 3, 2005, http://www.mothersmovement.org/features/05/h_hewett_1005/opting_out_print.htm.

4 Ralph Gardner, Jr., "Mom vs. Mom," *New York,* Oct. 21, 2002.

5 Ibid.

6 Miriam Peskowitz, *The Truth Behind the Mommy Wars: Who Decides What Makes A Good Mother?* (New York: Seal Press, 2005).

7 Judith Warner, "The Opt-Out Generation Wants Back In," *New York Times,* Aug. 7, 2013.

8 Sylvia Ann Hewlett and Carolyn Buck Lace, "Off-Ramps and On-Ramps," *Harvard Business Review,* March 2005.

9 "Life and Leadership after HBS," Harvard Business School, May 2015.

10 "Millennials in the Workplace Reinforcements, Not Trophies," Pew Research Center, April 12, 2016.

11 Jody Greenstone Miller and Matt Miller, "The Rise of the Supertemp," *Harvard Business Review,* May 2012.

CHAPTER 12: WHAT'S YOUR STORY?

1 Meredith Levo, "Do You Feel Like a Fraud? You Might Have the Impostor Syndrome," March 28, 2014, http://www.levo.com/articles/career-advice/female-boss-impostor-syndrome.

Index

Snyder, Kieran
  on gender differences, 26–27
social media
  branding with, 164, 175–177
  Hillary Clinton's use of, 22–23
  importance of using, 110
  and serendipity, 59–60
social serendipity, 56–57
"Sorry" (Beyoncé), 15
"Sorry Not Sorry: My Apology
  Addiction" (Lena Dunham),
  15–16
South by Southwest (SXSW)
  Interactive Conference,
  51–52
Sow, Aminatou
  on serendipity, 58–63
Spira, Jessica
  on opting in, 189–193
sponsors, 197
sports, women in, 25–26
Stahl, Leslie
  on motherhood, 180
Star, Darren, 110–111
"Starting from the Bottom"
  (Kathryn Minshew), 88
Star Trax (app), 206
The Start-Up of You (Reid Hoffman),
  82
Stern, Lyss
  on branding, 163–166
stigma, of failure, 127–128
strategic serendipity, 57–58
stresses, and hormone levels, 32
success, and confidence, 41–42
Sun, Lisa
  on her mother, 73
superconnectors, 80–81
Supergluemom blog, 150–151
sweetgreen, 9
SXSW (South by Southwest)
  Interactive Conference,
  51–52

Tannen, Deborah
  on double bind, 18–19

Tatum, Lisa Skeete
  on discomfort, 160
  on opting in, 195–197
tech industry
  and gender, 123, 125
  perception of failure in, 46
Tech LadyMafia, 60–61, 63, 64
"Telling It Like It Is" (Heather
  Hewett), 180–181
testosterone, 32
Texts from Hillary Clinton, 22
TheLi.st, 78–79
The Tipping Point (Malcolm
  Gladwell), 80–81
Title IX, 25–26
Today (television show), 155
Trump, Donald, 19–20
The Truth Behind the Mommy Wars
  (Miriam Peskowitz),
  182–183
Tsavo Media, 206
Tuite, Kathleen, 4–5
2016 presidential campaign,
  19–20, 22–24
20/20 (television program), 50

unconventional employment,
  108–110
Unplug Meditation, 139–144

value over replacement player
  (VORP), 100
video blogging, 156
virtual networking, 79
Vongalis-Macrow, Athena
  on networking, 83
VORP (value over replacement
  player), 100

Wake Forest University,
  89, 93
Walker, Alice
  on power, 29
Warner, Judith
  on opting out, 183–184
Wash + Fold, 37